Old-Time FIDDLE STYLE

A Collection of 35 Traditional Appalachian Tunes

By Ken Kolodner
with illustrations by Renee Baldwin

www.melbay.com/21992BCDEB

Audio Contents

1-3 Barlow Knife (pg. 22)
4-6 Big Sciota (pg. 23)
7-9 Booth Shot Lincoln (pg. 24)
10-12 Charles Guiteau (pg. 25)
13-15 Charleston Gals (pg. 26)
16-18 Chinquapin Hunting (pg. 27)
19-21 Devil in the Strawstack (pg. 28)
22-24 Elk River Blues (pg. 29)
25-27 Flop Eared Mule (pg. 30)
28-30 Fly Around My Pretty Little Miss (pg. 31)
31-33 Gray Cat on an Old Tennessee Farm (pg. 32)
34-36 Hangman's Reel (pg. 33)
37-39 Hell Among the Stallions (pg. 34)
40-42 Home with the Girls in the Morning (pg. 35)
43-45 Journey to the Heartland (pg. 36)
46-48 Julianne Johnson (pg. 37)
49 Little Star (pg. 38) - *This is only played once*
50-52 Liza Jane (pg. 39)
53-55 Mike in the Wilderness (pg. 40)
56-58 Needle Case (pg. 41)
59-61 Puncheon Floor (pg. 42)
62-64 Quince Dillon's High D (pg. 43)
65-67 Ragtime Annie (pg. 44)
68-70 Richmond (pg. 45)
71-73 Road Dog (pg. 46)
74-76 Roscoe (pg. 47)
77-79 Sally in the Garden (pg. 48)
80-82 Sandy Boys (pg. 49)
83-85 Shady Grove (pg. 50)
86-88 Shove That Pigs Foot a Little Bit Further in the Fire (pg. 51)
89-91 Single Footin' Horse (pg. 52)
92-94 Spotted Pony (pg. 53)
95-97 Washington's March (pg. 54)
98-100 West Fork Gals (pg. 55)
101-103 Whiskey Before Breakfast (pg. 56)

The audio includes all tunes played three times: very slowly, at a modest tempo and near full tempo.

LCCN: 2010927987

1 2 3 4 5 6 7 8 9 0

Visit us on the Web at www.melbay.com — E-mail us at email@melbay.com

Acknowledgements

Thanks to Renee Baldwin for her wonderful illustrations, to my son Brad Kolodner for sound editing, my wife Alison Brown for editing, to Kathy Sandersen for her cover design and help in putting the book together. I am forever grateful to the countless musicians from whom I learned the tunes and bowing techniques.

Table of Contents

Acknowledgements 2

Introduction: about this book and companion recording 4

Issues in transcribing fiddle tunes 5

Old-time style: the importance of bowing in old-time fiddling 5

Common bowing techniques 6

Left-hand ornaments, chords, swing, vibrato, dynamics, tunings 12

Learning tunes by ear 15

Tune selection 19

For the new fiddler: difficulty of tunes quick reference 20

The tunes 22

Index of tunes 57

About the author 58

Introduction:
About this book and companion recording

My experience in teaching old-time fiddle has been that playing the tunes at slower speeds greatly facilitates the process of getting the notes, feeling, groove and the stylistic details of the music, especially the bowing. To help you learn the tunes, I play three versions of each tune separately tracked. First, I play each tune with as little ornamentation as possible and mostly without the use of drone strings or chords. I play each tune the second time adding in chords, drone notes and possibly some left hand ornamentation. Finally, I play each tune once or twice near or at full tempo. In the last version (and sometimes in the second version), I sometimes add in a few variations either in the melody, rhythm and/or the bowing. My hope is that you will be able to listen and add some of these variations to your playing once you master the basic tune.

There is software available to slow down tunes and maintain the pitch. So, why did I bother playing the tunes at different speeds? I have found that many players find it useful to hear a basic version of a tune and learn from a straightforward version, without chords, drones and ornamentation. Once comfortable with a more basic version, it usually becomes easier to add in the extras. Further, many students and players have suggested to me that the added convenience of having different versions would be useful, especially as a practice aid.

There is a cultural belief among many old-time fiddlers that written notation cannot possibly capture the full sense of a tune. While I absolutely agree, written music can still serve as a useful guide, especially for those trained as readers and for visual learners. I am a believer in listening as much as possible and that there is absolutely no substitute for listening to the tunes. But if the written music helps you get a piece faster, then why not use it!? Additionally, I am a big believer that learning bowing systems can greatly help a player develop the solid rhythm and groove that is so essential to old-time music. A big frustration for so many players is that they can get the notes but not the feeling of the music. It may seem counter-intuitive but I have found that using written music helps many players get the bowings much faster which in turn facilitates getting the feel of the music...as long as the player also listens! Thus, the primary focus of this endeavor was to present a few “default” bowing systems that will help you play most tunes that you are likely to encounter.

My main disclaimer is that the bowing systems presented here represent just a fraction of the many approaches to playing old-time music. With so many idiosyncratic and regional styles, it is difficult to argue that any one approach is the way to go. Every experienced fiddler has his or her own take on how to play a tune and whether to play it in a particular style, often imitating the player from whom they learned the tune. I make no attempt in this book and on the recording to play a specific style but rather capture a few ideas that are used broadly in many styles of old-time fiddling. My experience is that it usually takes learning about four to six tunes of each bowing system to really start to capture the feel of the approach. I hope that you view these ideas as starting points for further exploration from experienced players.

In recording the tunes, I did not play with a metronome. My reason was that I wanted the tunes to have a bit more life to them. Those things always slow down and speed up anyway, don’t they!?

Issues in transcribing fiddle tunes

Tune versions. The versions presented here tend to be *very* standard renderings. Some old-time players will refer to a common version of a tune as a "festival" version. For the most part, that is what I have offered on the recording and in this book

Variations in note choices and bowing. In most styles of fiddling, it is commonplace for fiddlers to play variations. I tried to write down the notes as I am most likely to play and bow the tunes. Nonetheless, the tune transcriptions should be thought of as a guide and not etched in stone. For the moderate tempo and up-to-tempo versions, I tried to maintain consistency but sometimes took liberties with both the bowing and the choice of notes.

Double stops and drone notes. To keep the transcriptions as simple and readable as possible, with few exceptions (e.g. "Little Star"), I did not write in the double stops or drone notes. I have strived to keep the transcriptions simple and readable to all players. As a consumer of tune books, I find it very distracting to read transcriptions with chords, drone notes and other ornamentation as it can be difficult to figure out what the actual tune is! Hopefully, you will be able to hear some of the additions to the tunes that are not written. I also have added comments to give you some guidance as to when to add chords and drone notes.

Chord progressions in old-time fiddling. Many old-time players are very particular about sticking primarily to major chords (I, IV, V chords) and maintain strident opposition to using minor chords in tunes that are in major keys. Most old-time players also have an aversion to the use of fancier chords such as secondary dominants and other chord substitutions. I recognize that my chord choices are not always "traditional" as I am much more willing to deviate from the standard progressions. However, in most of the transcriptions, I keep to conventional chord choices. The chords that I provide are offered as suggestions. Feel free to try out other options.

2/4 versus 4/4. There is some debate whether it is best to write out tunes with two counts or four counts to a measure. I have adopted the more broadly used convention of four counts to a measure. My primary reasoning is simply that most players find 4/4 easier to read.

Old-time style: the importance of bowing in old-time fiddling

When one asks many fiddlers "do you think about your bowing when you play?" or "how do you get that sound?" or "how do you bow that tune?" a common response is something along the lines of "I just do anything that sounds or feels right." Unfortunately, this does not help someone to reproduce the sound. Upon closer examination, I have found that almost all fiddlers have a number of "default" bowings or "licks" that they use. And while the bow direction may look totally random at first, many fiddlers combine multiple bowing ideas in various ways even within the same tune. Many fiddlers are often not aware that they are using various patterns over and over again in many of their tunes.

As a student and a teacher of old-time fiddling, it didn't take me long to figure out that there were an astounding number of ways to successfully bow a tune. But it took me a long while to realize that having a few "default" bowings can get you through nearly any tune.

In the written versions of the tunes included on these CDs, I have used default bowings. Like many fiddlers, I rarely play or bow a tune exactly the same way twice in a row. If I do play all the same notes over again, rarely would I use the same bowing every time. Changing your bowing within the same tune can vary the feel of the tune. Having a number of bowing tricks (or licks) to employ is ideal.

I have relied on default bowings here because it is generally prudent to nail down one way to bow a tune first before getting too adventurous. In writing out the tunes for this project, I have limited the bowing options to a few basic ideas which include Nashville shuffle (and the related slur 2 separate 2 bowing), 3-1 bowing, ghost bows, the "rock," slur 2-2 bowing, some long slurs and "saw" bowing (individual bows on each note). Rather than offer 20 or 30 different bowing ideas, I present a very limited number of bowing ideas that are relatively easy to master (for the most part) and use them over and over again in the transcriptions. Get these bowing ideas down and you will still have plenty of options. Go explore other bowing ideas from other players: there are endless methods to successfully bow a tune.

Common bowing techniques

Saw bowing

The simplest bowing system is to use individual bows for each note. This is typically called *saw stroke* or *saw bowing*. Some players use saw bowing as their primary bowing, only rarely inserting the occasional slur, such as at the beginning of a section for pick-up notes and often at the end of a part of a phrase. Most players use saw bowing in parts of tunes or reserve the bowing for particular tunes. I did not present many tunes with saw bowing only because it is very straightforward.

Nashville (basic) shuffle

For those totally new to fiddling, the Nashville shuffle in its simplest form is a great place to start. The bowing that is most commonly presented in books and by fiddle instructors is the *Nashville shuffle*. The Nashville shuffle is a very useful and relatively easy system to learn. It is a powerful system and can be used to play almost any tune.

In its simplest form, this bowing system looks just like saw bowing. The first note is a quarter note followed by two eighth notes. Each note gets a single stroke. Many players like to think of this bowing as "long-short-short, long-short-short, etc." Since the bow direction changes with every note, the long is variously a down bow and then an up bow (i.e. DOWN-UP-DOWN and then UP-DOWN-UP). This bowing pattern puts a down bow on the beginning note of a measure (the "down beat" or the "one" count of a measure of four.)

There is a natural tendency to want to accent the quarter notes. That is, we naturally tap our foot and accent on the "one" and "three" counts of a measure—i.e. ONE—two—THREE—four). However, many players instead consciously try to shift the accents to the first of each pair of the eighth notes, thereby putting a pulse on the "back beat" or the "two and four" counts. Thus, we play a longer bow on the quarter notes on "one" and "three" but accent "one-TWO-and-three-FOUR-and." Another way to think of the accent on the two and four counts is "long-SHORT-short, long-SHORT-short." This is perhaps a preferable way to accent. Even better is to shift your accent patterns so that while you are mostly hitting the two and four counts, you periodically shift to one and three.

For an example of the Nashville shuffle in its simplest form, see "Gray Cat on an Old Tennessee Farm." A second very easy example is "Barlow Knife" and a third is "Flop Eared Mule." I have included the basic Nashville shuffle in some more difficult tunes such as "Home with Girls in Morning," "Road Dog" and "Journey to the Heartland."

"Nashville shuffle" or the basic shuffle (long-short-short)

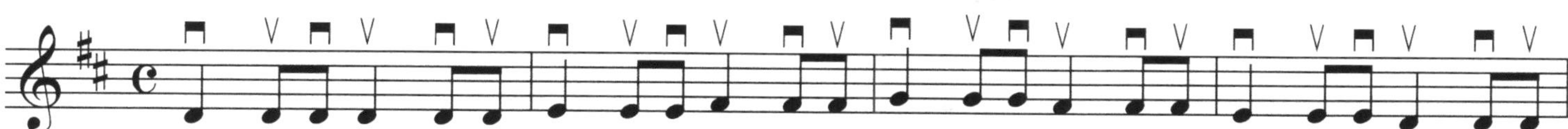

A slight extension of the simplest form of the Nashville shuffle is to add a double stop using an adjacent open string on the first pair of each eighth note. This "touch" of the adjacent string occurs on the "two" and "four" counts of a measure (the back beat) and will provide a natural accenting that is desirable in many tunes. This bowing still requires that the "touch" alternately occurs with down and up bows. It is a bit tricky to add this "touch" chord but this is an excellent second bowing to master. You will see later that there are perhaps more convenient alternatives to this bowing system. I use it in many of the tunes where I have the simple shuffle as the bowing system. However, I rarely use the "touch" for more than a few measures or perhaps a section of the tune.

"Nashville shuffle" with a drone string (double stop) on the "two" and "four" count

The Nashville shuffle works just fine when encountering a pattern of one quarter followed by two eighth notes. And this is a common rhythm in fiddle tunes. When we are confronted with four or more eighth notes in succession, the Nashville shuffle still works but requires a slurring pattern. Imagine a measure of all eighth notes. We now slur the first two eighth notes and separate the next two notes and do the same pattern for the next four eighth notes. The bow direction is exactly equivalent to the original Nashville shuffle when we had one quarter followed by two eighth notes. Again, the bow direction on the slurred notes alternates between up and down bows. Some refer to this bowing as "slur two, separate two" bowing. But it is really just the simple Nashville shuffle in disguise. See again "Barlow Knife" for one measure of this usage (in the B and C parts), "Journey to the Heartland," "Home with the Girls in the Morning," and "Road Dog."

"Nashville shuffle" with eighth notes: "slur two" and "separate two"

We can extend this bowing so that a touch of the adjacent string occurs on the first pair of each bow separated eighth notes. And this again occurs on the two and four counts of each measure. Thus, we simply play a drone string or a chord but limit doing so only on the two and four counts. This touching of the drone or a chord on the two and four counts is a somewhat more difficult bowing to master but still well worth the effort. Alternately, drone strings can be added on all of these variants of the Nashville shuffle.

"Nashville shuffle" with eighth notes and chords (double stops) on the two and four counts: "slur two" and "separate two"

"3-1" or "Circle" or "Georgia shuffle" bowing

The Nashville shuffle and its related extensions are very useful bowing systems and can be used in nearly all tunes. But it is by far not my preferred way of bowing most tunes. I probably use it in 15-20% of my tunes. If I were to pick one bowing system to use over and over again, it would perhaps be some variant of "3-1" bowing." This is sometimes called the Georgia Shuffle. (There are many variants of the Georgia Shuffle such as a pattern of 1-1-1-3-1-1 or other patterns where a slur of 3 is introduced, assuming we are playing all eighth notes.) This bowing system involves a series of slurring three notes followed by a single bow. The basic idea is that the single bow is always played on the two and four counts. Imagine a few measures of all eighth notes. We could start with a down bow slurring the first two notes, followed by a single up, followed by a down slur of three, followed by a single up, followed by a down slur of three, followed by a single up, etc.

With "3-1" bowing, note the sequences of a slur of three notes followed by a single up bow. We start with a slur of two notes only to get the first up bow on the "two" count. The 3-1 pattern is seen more clearly once we have a longer succession of 8th notes.

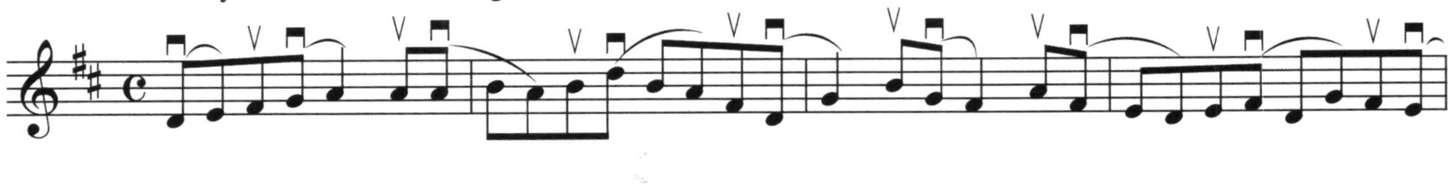

Since three eighth notes are played with a single slur and so that you don't run out of bow, you must play the next eighth note with a much faster stroke. The faster bow speed occurs on the two and four counts and creates the lift. Many players also bow the two and four a bit harder than the slurred notes but mostly it is the accelerated speed of the bow that creates the lift. This bowing system provides great lift and once you get the idea, you fall into a rhythmic pattern that (eventually) is easy to feel and remember. If pressed to describe the difference in feel between the Nashville and Georgia shuffles, I offer this: While the Nashville shuffle can provide a suitable back beat pulse on the 2 and 4, the Georgia shuffle will create the effect with a much smoother and more relaxed feel. The Nashville shuffle might naturally possess a bit more drive but the Georgia shuffle tends to provide a more natural pulse and a lighter lift. It feels more danceable to me. The key is that the bowing system adds pulse to the tunes. Both bowing systems do that but 3-1 bowing tends to have a more natural groove.

When using 3-1 bowing, most players use an up bow on the slur of three notes and a down bow on the single note on the two and four counts. Many players will strongly debate this point but I believe that it doesn't really matter which way one goes. In fact, I typically prefer to reverse this such that the "slur three" is typically down and the single bow is up. I will often go both ways within the same tune just for fun (placing the up bow on the two and four and then switching to a down bow on the two and four). It does have a slightly different feel somehow. Learning to go both ways seems ideal to me. I've heard some refer to this bowing as "circle" bowing because the right hand appears to make a bit of a circular motion once it launches into a series of consecutive 3-1 patterns. Because this is such a useful pattern to learn, I use it in many of the tunes presented here.

One can completely reverse the bow direction and get the same basic effect. Note that a down bow occurs on the two and four counts.

Below are some variants of this bowing pattern. Note that the up bows remain on the counts of two and four.

"Circle" bowing--you can completely reverse the bow direction and get the same basic effect. Note that an up bow occurs on the two and four counts. This is contrast to the simplest form of the Nashville shuffle where the ups and downs can occur on any count.

"Circle" bowing with double stops on adjacent open string which again adds emphasis on the off-beats (the "2 and 4" counts).

"Slur 2" and "rocking" as a string-crossing technique

Slurring pairs of two eighth notes can be an effective bowing especially for communicating a smooth "swing." I often use it for small passages in tunes as an alternative to the groove oriented bow patterns of 3-1 and Nashville shuffle. I sometimes use it for entire tunes. An example of this bowing is in the B part of "Washington's March."

A "slur two" pattern creates a smooth but rhythmic bowing.

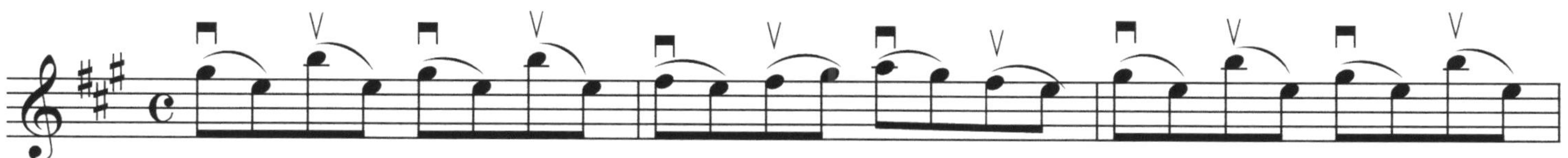

One of the challenges in fiddling is effective "string-crossing" (moving back and forth in succession from one string to the next.) Many players tend to over-shoot until they realize relatively small movements are most conducive to successful string-crossing. There are a variety of effective bowing strategies for string-crossing. Many players simply alternate saw bowing (single strokes) back and forth. This works just fine. However, one of the more pleasing string-crossing bowing approaches is to "rock" using a slur-2 pattern. Typically, the slur begins on a note on a higher string and moves to a note on a lower string, always in pairs of two notes, creating a rocking feeling. Hence the bowing is sometimes called "rocking." It is not easy to execute this bowing as there is a tendency to use more motion than is necessary. But once you get the hang of it, it is a great tool. Examples of the "rock" are plentiful and include the C part of "Journey to the Heartland," the B part of "Puncheon Floor" and "Devil in the Strawstack" and in the A part of "Ragtime Annie."

"Saw" bowing (the first two measures) can be a bit choppy but can be used effectively for string crossing. An alternative for string crossing is to "rock" where notes are slurred in pairs of two, slurring from the higher to the lower string (the last two measures).

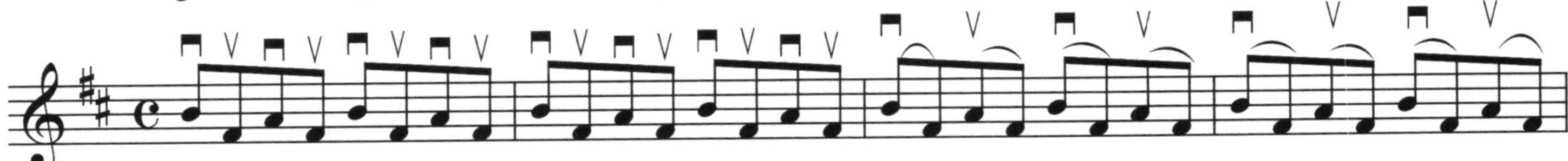

Interestingly, this bowing can be used very effectively as an alternative to the Nashville shuffle, ghosting and other shuffles. For example, in the B part of "Puncheon Floor," the first several measures could be played with a straight Nashville shuffle where each quarter note would be followed by two eighth notes, all with separate bows. Alternately, one might use a Georgia shuffle. I like to vary this section using both of these bowing ideas and also use a slur-two pattern as I have written it.

"Ghost" bows

"Ghosting" is a wonderful bowing technique that is essential to master at some point in your fiddling career! In many of the tune transcriptions, you will see two or more up bows in a row (e.g. the A part of "Mike in the Wilderness," the B part of "Charles Guiteau.") Occasionally, fiddlers will do two up bows or down bows with a brief stop in the bowing, continuing in the same bow direction. A more common technique is to insert a very lightly played down bow in between the two up bows. It is played with a "whisper" of a bow, played so lightly that it is only audible when played slowly but not when played up to tempo. Ghost bows provide lightness in phrasing that must be experienced or heard to fully appreciate. I have not indicated ghost bows in the transcriptions but generally it is safe to assume that a ghost bow should be played whenever you encounter two or more up bows in a sequence. There are exceptions (e.g. see measure 3 in the A part of "Julianne Johnson" where two ups are indicated but I do not use a ghost in between the notes). Hopefully, you will be able to hear the difference in the phrasing when I am playing two up bows with no ghost in between versus using a ghost bow. And if you do happen to play a ghost bow, it really will not matter. It just colors the phrasing differently. When in doubt, use a ghost bow!

To suggest the "ghost" bow, I have inserted a down bow stroke but no note! Thus, in between a sequence of two or more up bows is a down bow that is played without producing much if any sound. The bow is not lifted off the string but rather is played extremely lightly.

"Mid-bow" pulse

The idea with a mid-bow pulse is to play two notes of the same pitch, or give the appearance of two notes, with a single bow without changing the bow direction and without stopping your bow. A mid-bow pulse may be used to change a half note into two quarter notes of the same pitch, rather than changing the bow direction or stopping your bow. A mid-bow pulse may also be used for a dynamic change in a note or simply to change the emphasis in a single note. I do not notate these.

"Anticipations"

"Anticipation" is a technique used in many styles of fiddling and especially in old-time music. Some players refer to anticipations as "jump beats." This is an appropriate term as the basic idea is that we *jump* early to a specific count in the music. Typically, an anticipation occurs by pulling whatever is supposed to occur on the "one count" of a measure into the preceding "four" count or the "four and" count of the preceding measure. The anticipation may occur exactly on the "four" count or the "four and" count or somewhere in between or just after either count. It is totally up to the player where the anticipation begins. The idea is that you simply arrive to the "one" count early. A very frequent use of anticipation is to replace pick-up notes at the beginning of an A or B part of the tune with the first note of the first measure that follows: we use a single bow stroke to tie from the pickup measure into the downbeat into the first note of the measure. I often debate whether I should notate anticipations or leave it up to the individual player to determine when to add an "anticipation." In some cases, I have written out the anticipations such as in the second measure of the B part of "Sandy Boys." In general, I have not written these out as it tends to make the reading of the tune a bit harder. Many fiddlers use the technique in nearly every tune. Anticipations are an integral part of old-time fiddling.

Measures one and two show an example of an anticipation. Measures three and four show the same phrase without the anitcipation. The basic idea is to arrive at the E "early" by pulling the note from the "one" count in measure two and play it instead approximately on the "four" count in the preceding measure.

Recovery bows

A common practice is to add a note or two and consequently a bow stroke to facilitate the execution of a bowing pattern. Fiddlers commonly add these "extra" notes at the end of an A or B part but they can occur anywhere. Some fiddlers call these bow strokes "recoveries." For example, see the last note of the alternate B part of "Spotted Pony" and the last note of "Whiskey Before Breakfast."

Bow direction

Many fiddlers have strong feelings about bow direction. By far, the prevailing belief is that the down bow is naturally more powerful. For this reason, some players insist on placing a down bow on the "one" count of each measure. While the down bow may feel more powerful, others argue that the up bow can provide a nice "lift." The direction you prefer in a given tune may be at least partially determined by the desired effect. Many players have a preference to either go up or down on certain counts in the tune. For example, in "3-1 bowing" (where one slurs a group of three eighth notes followed by a single bow for one eighth note), I tend to use up bows on the 2 and 4 counts. But one could easily reverse completely the bow direction and produce a similar sound and feel. In fact, I do this often where I simply reverse my bowings. Most fiddlers reverse this pattern. Some players believe that you should be able to create the same effect either with a down or up bow.

The bottom-line is that while I hope that you try them out, none of the suggested bowings are etched in stone. For example, you may try reversing the bowings to see if they work better for you. Almost any bowing can work as long as you can maintain a solid rhythm and feel for the tunes.

Variations in bowing and melody

In mastering even a few different bowing ideas, one gains the potential to incorporate many bowing ideas in a single tune. A great way to vary one's playing is to learn to simply vary one's bowing within a tune. For example, you might use 3-1 bowing throughout most of a tune and then play instead a Nashville shuffle and saw bowing for a few measures. For example, I briefly use Nashville shuffle in measure three of the B part in "Hell Among the Stallions." In "Home with the Girls in the Morning," we start with Nashville shuffle but switch to 3-1 bowing on the ending measures. Or you might move from 3-1 bowing to "slur two" bowing or a rock (see "Washington's March" which switches from slur-two to 3-1). Any change in bowing is subtle to most listeners but makes a big difference in the phrasing of the tune. The trick is to not lose your groove as ultimately all bowing patterns are intended to provide a rhythmic foundation to a tune. Since I have written out the tunes only once, in order to keep things simple, I primarily used default bowings and have explicitly not mixed bowings in one tune. However, feel free to mix and match as much as you can, but only once you get the hang of each bowing system. The reality is that many players tend to mix up their bowing as a way to vary their playing.

One of the great joys in playing old-time music is that most players feel quite free to change the melody upon playing the tune multiple times. I like to think of tunes as having "skeletons" which form the heart of the piece. Many of the other notes in the tune are really not that vital to the integrity of the piece. Some musicians call the essential notes of the tune "anchors" or "corners." A basic concept in improvisation is to keep the corners or the anchors of the tune in tact but everything else is fair game. Some players also keep the skeleton of the tune running in their heads and improvise primarily using the chord progression. Improvisation and creating tune variations in old-time tunes is great fun but it is really too big of a topic to treat here fairly. Similarly, in the recorded and transcribed versions, I have resisted the temptation to do much in the way of either varying the tunes or the bowing. I tried to play the tunes in a fairly consistent way.

Left-hand ornaments, chords, swing, vibrato, dynamics, tunings

Left-hand ornaments—slides, hammer-ons, triplets, fourth finger unisons, dissonances, "wild" notes

While the focus of most old-time fiddlers is generally on establishing the groove (and therefore bowing) and not on left-hand ornamentation, there are nonetheless many ideas that players use.

Sliding into (up) and out of notes (down) is a very common technique. For example, when the melody goes from the first finger to the open string (e.g. moving down from an F sharp to an open string E), many players will slide *down* from the first note into the open string. Alternately, we can slide *up* when the melody moves from an open string to the first finger (e.g. E to F sharp).

Sliding into and out of a unison of the fourth finger and open string is also a very common idea and is an absolute must to be mastered! The effect is a movement of dissonance to consonance and back to dissonance as the player slides in and out of the unison. The fourth finger creation of dissonance is used widely. As an example, let's say that the melody notes are two half-notes of a high E. Easiest is to play an open string E with two bow strokes. A bit more challenging is to use the fourth finger on the A string to obtain the E. Most of the time, it is best to do both! While playing the open string E, we use the fourth finger and slide down from the unison E down to around a D sharp and back up to the E, often using a single bow for the whole measure. An alternate method is to use the fourth finger for the unison but drop to a third finger for a temporary dissonance against the higher string and then return to the unison note. Other times, you might hold the unison and use a first finger for a quick unison against the fourth finger. (You will sometimes see players use their third finger instead of their fourth finger to produce unisons.) For classical players taught to avoid open strings, just forget all that. Open strings are to be cherished, especially as drone strings but also to be used with 4th finger unisons. (When using altered tunings, the third finger is often used for unisons. The effect is still the same.)

Other effects include various grace notes, hammer-ons, bowed and slurred triplets (both up and down), "wild notes" and other ideas. For clarity of the notation, I rarely notated these techniques. My hope is that you will be able to hear them and reproduce them. Wild notes are ambiguous notes that are "in between" notes (e.g., in between a C natural and C sharp) and are used intentionally by some players. I did not use them on this recording.

Chords: use of open (drone) adjacent strings and double-stops

A very common practice in old-time fiddling is to add an open adjacent string to the melody line. This produces a fair amount of dissonance which is considered to be a highly desired effect. Still, fiddlers will choose a drone string that generally fits the chords of the tune. My experience is that many fiddlers have a limited knowledge of chords. Instead, most fiddlers simply use their ears to guide the best choice of which string to use (below or above the melody). It becomes rather intuitive after playing for a while.

Still, knowing something about chords is very useful not just to choose drone strings but also to add other double-stops (fingering two notes on two different strings). There are countless benefits in learning about chord progressions. For example, it makes learning tunes much easier if you can "see" the chords as tunes are often combinations of arpeggios and scale patterns. Your chord choices will be informed and not conflict with guitarists and you will be able to communicate with others much better. Further, surviving in jams is much easier when you can follow a chord progression.

Playing chords is one the great pleasures in fiddling. Obviously, a prerequisite is that you are able to play two strings at the same time. Some players think that they have to play harder (using more bow pressure) in order to play two strings at once. This is not at all true. I like to remind students that there are seven "planes" (or bow angles) to learn on the fiddle. Of course, we have the four strings. And we also have three pairs of adjacent strings. That totals seven. Before attempting chords, one must be comfortable moving through the seven planes. Next, you have to have the ability to play a scale along with an open drone string. This can be challenging at first, especially if your fingers are flattening out on the strings. Keep your fingers nicely curled and you should be able to master this eventually. Some players "cheat" by tilting their fingers slightly to the open string that they are *not* using as a drone. This can work well but, eventually, it is good to simply learn to get your fingers to cleanly play on one string only and not touch the other strings (except when barring two strings with a single finger.)

When first introduced to fiddling, sometimes classically-trained violinists resist using open strings in favor of the fourth finger. While the fourth finger is great to use (as discussed above, especially for unisons with an adjacent higher open string), it is time to relax! The open strings are frequently used as drone notes. Most old-time fiddlers will use a drone string constantly through a tune. It is simply my preference to add a little contrast by playing at least parts of most tunes without adding a drone string. The main exception is that drone strings are typically used almost all the time in cross-tuning. After all, that is one of the great advantages of cross-tuning as any drone string will work all the time. For readability of the transcriptions, I did not write in either drone notes and occasionally wrote in two-tone chords (double-stops). I hope that you can hear the addition of the drone strings plus I often added comments about which string to use.

Swing

One of the big issues especially for those new to old-time fiddling is the concept of swing. Swing results from the uneven spacing of eighth notes whereby the first note is held longer than the second pair of each eighth note. Another way to think of swing is that the eighth notes are played with a slight "dotted" rhythm. For readability, however, tunes are almost never written out to suggest swing. Rather, it is best to hear a tune played in order to find an appropriate amount of swing.

Stepping out on a limb, the question is really not "to swing or not to swing" but simply how much one should swing in a given tune. In a jamming situation or when playing with other fiddlers, I try to modify my swing to fit the general sound. For example, if I am playing with a player who plays with a lot of swing, I will try to match it to find their groove. However, if a player uses with very little swing, again I may accommodate and match their swing or perhaps we will find a middle ground. If a fiddler plays very stiffly with no swing, that is a problem as it is likely to be difficult to feel the groove. For passages within a given tune, I sometimes will play with very little swing but rarely will I do so throughout an entire tune.

Vibrato

Vibrato is universally *not* used by old-time fiddlers and is widely frowned upon. It sometimes slips into my playing. I offer my apologies! Please ignore my occasional lapses.

Dynamics

Do dynamics belong in old-time music? I definitely think so and endeavor to play dynamically. However, my intent in recording these tunes was to communicate the bowing and phrasing of the tunes. I intentionally mostly played the tunes with a very flat dynamic just to make it easier to hear the tunes at a constant level. On the fast versions, you might hear some dynamics happening. In general, for instructional purposes, I did not communicate dynamics on the CD. However, I prefer to *not* blast away at the same volume through an entire tune.

Tunings

Many old-time fiddlers live to play tunes in altered tunings and often have fiddles that remain in "cross-tuning" or some other tuning all the time. Many other players never re-tune. Why re-tune? Perhaps the primary reason is that one can obtain different colors and dissonances only in the various tunings. The second is that some tunes are simply easier to play in the tunings. A third reason is that many tunes that can be played on the top two strings can be moved to the bottom two strings using the same fingering when cross-tuned (e.g., A-E-A-E or G-D-G-D). Fourth, some of the tunings produce more volume of sound because of the sympathetic sound produced by the tuning. Frequent or constant use of adjacent drone strings contribute to this greater sound. (Sometimes people will hear a cross-tuned fiddle and say "wow, it sounds like two fiddles!") In cross-tuning, open string drones work with the melody no matter whether you are above the melody or below the melody as your choice of the drone string: i.e. any string will work making one's playing of drone strings simultaneously very mindless and pleasing! Deciding which drone string to use is basically up to you in terms for which sounds best. Many tunes just sound so much better played in the various tunings. It does take some getting used to in order to play in an altered tuning since the intervals will be different between strings. You will have to re-train your fingers, especially when reading the transcriptions (which are notated in standard tuning)!

There are many altered tunings used by old-time players. Foremost is "cross-tuning" in A-E-A-E. Re-tune the G string to an A and the D string to an E. Although it is extremely unlikely to break a string doing this (unless you go too far beyond the A or E), many people are nervous about tuning up. An alternative is to tune to G-D-G-D. This produces a darker sound but it is equivalent to A-E-A-E in terms of your fingering. On this recording, I use A-E-A-E for all the tunes in the key of A but one could just as well play all A-E-A-E tunes in G-D-G-D. Most old-time fiddlers cross-tune for nearly all tunes when playing in the key of A and A mixolydian. Another fairly common tuning used for the key of A is A-E-A-C sharp.

For the key of D, many players stay in standard tuning but a very common alternative is to tune the G string up to an A, resulting in A-D-A-E. Instead of using the (dreaded) fourth finger on the low string, the third finger conveniently takes it place, making it easier to play a unison with the D string. The bigger advantage (if you consider avoiding the fourth finger an advantage) is simply that you can obtain some dissonances and drones that were otherwise not easily obtained without retuning. Further, sometimes you can drop entire sections of tunes that reside on the upper strings down to the lower octave. Other D tunings include A-D-A-D and D-D-A-D. In A-D-A-D, the lowered E string allows for some very nice effects. I use it on this recording in "Washington's March" and sometimes on "Home with the Girls in Morning." On this recording, I did not play in D-D-A-D but it is wonderful tuning. It can be a challenge to keep the low D in tune but it is worth the effort.

If you are new to playing in altered tunings, sight-reading can be a challenge. It may be easier to first play the tune in standard tuning to get the sense of the piece. Better yet is to listen to the tune a lot before trying to play it. Once you start to work on the tune, don't worry about the bowing. After you have played the tune at least a few times through and basically have the idea of the tune, then re-tune and try it out. Let your ears guide your fingers. Ultimately, I find it easier to use the ears especially for altered tunings and not rely on the written music, except to get the bowing.

Learning tunes by ear

You may choose to ignore the tune transcriptions, develop your own bowings and try to learn the tunes totally by ear. Improving your listening skills is vitally important, especially as fiddlers! I offer this next discussion to encourage you to develop your ear.

Shortly after finishing college and just before heading to graduate school, I decided that I would teach myself to play the fiddle. I had no music background and didn't read music. I tuned the fiddle using a pitch pipe (bad idea), bought a few albums (remember those round things?) from County Records of old-time fiddle "classics" and proceeded to listen to the tunes over and over again. It was a total struggle, my technique was non-existent and I really had no clue what I was doing. But, in time, I did begin to approximate what I heard on the recordings. I can't honestly say that I would recommend trying to take the road that I went. If I had it to do all over, I would have found a teacher, focused on technique and, yes, learned to read music *and* learned some music theory right from the start. But the process of learning solely with my ears forced me to listen and perhaps gain some appreciation of what old-time fiddling was "supposed" to sound like.

My experience is that an overwhelming majority of the more accomplished players of traditional music believe very strongly that to fully understand the phrasing of the music, learning by ear and from experienced players is much preferred to learning solely from sheet music. While it may be true that the subtleties of the music cannot be effectively notated (e.g. swing, anticipations, ornamentations etc…), once you become an experienced player, written music can be an important aid in expediting learning tunes. I have a very large library of traditional music books and often learn tunes by reading. Experienced players can often interpret written music and create a version of the tune that sounds "traditional." Over the years, I have become a strong believer in getting as many people participating in playing music as possible and doing whatever it takes to get everyone going. This means that written music is a useful aid. Nevertheless, there are many advantages and situations when learning by ear is a great asset. There is simply no substitute for developing your ears.

The issue is really not whether there is significant value in learning traditional music by ear. The bigger issue is how does one learn to master the skill of listening and learning by ear? I hope that some of the techniques discussed below will help you in your quest to practice learning by ear. Many of the ideas are obvious but they still bear mentioning. As with any other skill, the more understanding you have and the more techniques you bring to the process, the more likely are your chances for success.

Ten "Tools of the Trade"

(1.) **Identify the meter.** In old-time music, you are almost guaranteed that every tune that is played in a jam will be in 4/4. Old-time musicians do not play jigs (6/8) but do play the occasional waltz (3/4). Still, viewing the broader world of learning by ear, we need to establish the meter of the tune. There are some tunes that do not stay in a consistent meter. These are among the tunes that are said to be "crooked." Crooked tunes might have an extra count to a measure or a full extra measure in an A or B part of the tune. It can take a while to understand these tunes—repeated listening usually gets you there.

(2.) **Find the tonal center and understanding the modes.** Find the note on which the tune resolves. This is a great start to get you rolling as this *might* (probably) tell you which key the tune resides but be careful. It is better to understand the "modes" as most traditional music is typically in one of four modes. The modes tell you where to play physically, what notes to expect, and the chords that you are most likely to encounter.

Most common is what we will all know as major but is also known in mode-speak as Ionian. Don't skip this section and start rolling your eyes! The other modes can easily be found by starting on different notes of the major scale and playing eight notes. First, let's start on the second note of the major scale and form a scale called the Dorian mode. It might sound a little weird to play this scale. I did not include any tunes in Dorian but don't let that fool you—it is a very common mode. The tonal center uses a minor chord. Thus, the mode sounds minor.

Now, let's skip to the fifth note of a major scale and form the mixolydian mode. Players often misclassify this mode and call it major. That is probably because the mode has a major chord for its tonal center. But the mode does not sound like it is in a major key and has a sort of, well, "modal" sound! (See "Mike in the Wilderness," "Sandy Boys".) Next, from the sixth note, we form the Aeolian mode. This is also called the "relative minor" (See "Devil in the Strawstack," "Home with the Girls in the Morning," most of "Journey to the Heartland," and "Sally in the Garden"). There are many tunes that switch modes from one part to the next. For example, a common usage is to move from major to relative minor (Aeolian).

People will often say "this tune is modal." This really doesn't mean much since all traditional tunes are modal! If you can learn how the modes work and recognize them, this can be a huge clue into finding the notes of tune faster since you will know which scale to use. Tunes typically are composed of scalar patterns and pieces of chords (arpeggios). Once you find the correct mode, you will at least have a frame of reference from which to get started.

(3.) **Think structure.** Identify the number of parts that a tune has and within each part, the number of phrases. Most importantly, phrases usually repeat, and sometimes phrases repeat multiple times within a tune. Most tunes have two parts: an "A" and "B" section. Within these parts, most tunes are composed in two measure phrases with a question and answer format. While many different structures are common, a very typical construction of phrases is as follows.

The A part: (Phrase A1) A two measure "question"
(Phrase A2) A two measure "answer"
(Phrase A1) Repeat question #1
(Phrase A3) A new two measure answer (the ending)

The B part: (Phrase B1) A new question
(Phrase B2) A new answer or possibly the first answer of the A part (A2)
(Phrase B1) Repeat the new question
(Phrase A3) The ending of the A part or possibly a new answer (B3).

Another way to think of this construction is to imagine a conversation that goes as follows:
Question/statement: "Hey?!"
Answer: "What?!"
Repeat the question/statement: "I said 'Hey?!'"
New answer: "OK!"

There are many good examples of this exact construction (see "Needle Case," "Single Footin' Horse" and many others.) But watch for the occasional crooked tune!

(4.) **Think chord progressions.** My ability to learn tunes by ear improved enormously once I began to understand chord progressions. Now, I cannot imagine learning a tune without first identifying a basic chord structure (not necessarily "the" chord progression but at least a likely or "beginning" chord progression). Identifying the modes and a "beginning" chord structure are integrally related. This is an enormous topic which regrettably is beyond the scope of this discussion. I would encourage you to learn the four big modes and learn which chords commonly occur in each of them. It bears repeating that tunes are essentially scalar fragments (pieces of scales) and arpeggiated chords (pieces of chords) put together in clever ways. Once you see that, you can find tunes much faster.

(5.) **Simplify: Identify *target* or *anchor* notes or phrases**. Almost every tune has what some musicians call variously the "corners," "anchors" or "target notes" that are critical to defining the tune. To new players, it can be a mystery why there are so many versions of common tunes. They often want to know what the "real" tune is. Or maybe they might complain "that is not the way you wrote it down!" or "that isn't the way it is in the book!" The reality is that many notes in most tunes are relatively unimportant and that there may be only a few phrases or critical notes within each phrase that are essential to the integrity of the tune. These are the "anchors" of the tune. A typical technique in learning by ear is to find these notes first and then gradually fill out the tune upon repeated listening. Some musicians call this finding the "skeleton" of the tune. In many tunes, you discover that a good part of the melody is not that critical to the tune, but the tune must have the anchors, corners or whatever you want to call them. In other words, you can create your own version of the tune as long as it is reasonably close to what you are hearing and you retain the anchors. Do not get lost in the details of the less important notes. If you don't like a few note choices in my tune versions, feel free to change them!

(6.) **Practice and learn intervals.** Even if you do not think chords or even modes, being able to recognize intervals is perhaps the key to figuring out tunes, once you identify the structure. Identifying the mode/key is certainly very important, and identifying the chords is a huge bonus. But recognizing intervals can get you very far. Formal ear training typically consists of learning the distances between any two notes (intervals). Many of us practice scales up and down. This is not sufficient. At a minimum:

(a.) practice playing thirds through major scales (e.g. the key of D, walk up the scale playing D - F sharp; E - G; F sharp - A; G - B; A - C sharp; B - D; C sharp - E; D - F sharp; and then go back down: E - C sharp; D - B; C sharp - A; B - G; A - F sharp; G - E; F sharp - D) and

(b.) practice arpeggios and their inversions all over the instrument, backwards and forwards.

and

(c.) learn to recognize other intervals (fourths, sixths etc.).

Why do all of this? Again, most tunes are comprised of scalar patterns, little sections of movement in thirds, mini arpeggios in their various forms in all directions, and so on. In addition to using the above practice tools, there are all sorts of simple ways to recognize the many intervals you are likely to encounter. Using examples of common tunes is perhaps the easiest. For example,

For a "minor third," think the first two notes of "Greensleeves"
For a fifth down, think "Flint-stones" (ok, you have to be a certain age for that one)
For a fifth up, think "Twinkle, Twinkle"
For a fourth up, think "A-amaze" in "Amazing Grace" or "Here Comes" in "Here Comes the Bride"
For a major arpeggio, use "Morning Has Broken" or "Soldier's Joy" or see measures 1-2 in "Elk River Blues," "Flop Eared Mule," "Quince Dillon's High D" and many other tunes in this book
For a sixth down, "Crazy" and the beginning of "Liberty"
For a sixth up, the beginning of "Bill Cheathum" or "It Came Upon A Midnight Clear" and see measure two in "Needle Case"
For an octave, "Some-where" in "Somewhere over the Rainbow" and see measure one in "Home with the Girls in the Morning"

You can find many others by simply trying out different common tunes. Practice playing the interval and learn to hear and recognize it.

(7.) **Practice learning small pieces at a time; practice "call and response."** If you listen to the entire tune over and over again, you risk getting overwhelmed. In a jamming situation, you have no choice. But this is NOT the place to start to develop the skill of learning by ear. You will likely sit there and be frustrated by sensory overload. Rather than listen to an entire piece over and over again, it really helps to take very small pieces of the tune and master only that. Practice that small piece and get it down before you move on. When working with a CD or other recording, I must admit that I sometimes write it down as I go (hitting the pause button!) just so that I can remember it later. I see no harm in doing so as you are still learning by ear! A common technique in teaching a tune is to use "call" and "response" where a phrase is played; perhaps a full two measures or perhaps smaller depending on what can be most easily digested. Try to play as much of the phrase as you can. The "call" and "response" is continued until the learner gets the whole phrase. Additional phrases are added using the same technique, gradually incorporating larger pieces until the whole tune is captured.

(8.) **Slow it down.** Experienced musicians sometimes disparage the practice of slow jams at festivals. I understand that this may not be the "traditional" way to learn. I understand that by slowing down the tunes significantly, there is a risk that the groove and other subtleties of the tunes are lost or obscured. The point of the slow jam or slowing the tune down is to get people to learn, have fun, and build confidence. Most of us do not find the time to listen and practice for hours. Nor do we often have access to other players. So I am all for playing the tunes slowly which is why I did this book with a recording! In fact, you can learn a lot by playing the tunes slowly and hearing them slowed down. For example, it is especially difficult for newer players to hear the "swing" in the tunes when played up to tempo.

(9.) **Learn from different instruments.** Since you are likely to want to learn tunes from all sorts of players and sources, try learning from an instrument other than the instrument you play. You can learn so much about the phrasing and other subtleties in the music by listening to experienced players of other instruments.

(10.) **Listen for subtleties in the music.** As you gain skill and experience learning by ear, hopefully your focus shifts to pick up the subtleties in the music. I always recommend that it is best when first learning a tune to basically ignore ornamentation and other details: i.e., simplify! But after I have the basic tune, I listen for details. Especially important is to listen for swing. As described earlier, fiddlers and other musicians typically speak of swing as the evenness (or lack thereof) of spacing of the eighth notes such that the first note of a pair of eighth notes is held longer than the second. Listen also for the accent shifts (e.g., in 4/4, the degree to which the pulse is on the two and four counts as opposed to one and three or possibly on the counts of "and"), anticipations and other ornamentation.

Misconceptions about learning by ear

I would like to offer a final word on several misconceptions about learning by ear. First, you do NOT need to be able to sing very well (or at all) to learn by ear. I hear it stated often that you need to be able to sing the tune in order to play it by ear. Singing the tune certainly helps many people but it is also not necessary. Rather, you only need to learn to "hear" the tune "in your head." Second, you do not need "perfect" pitch (e.g. you do not need to ever know what an "A" sounds like) but only need to develop a sense of "relative" pitch. Most musicians develop a sense of relative pitch—few have perfect pitch. Third, while some people are perhaps "naturals" and can hear tunes easily, learning by ear is a skill to be learned, practiced and developed. You will get better and better at learning by ear by practicing and understanding the many components of the task. Finally, learning by ear does not need to be "rote learning." Rote learning usually involves playing something over and over again typically without any thinking. Some people confuse learning by ear as rote learning—that you *just* have to listen many, many times to get a tune. And you *just* listen and play it over and over again until you memorize it. That might work for some or even many people. As I have tried to describe above, I would argue that for many of us there is clearly much more to the process, *especially* if you want to retain the tune for a long time. Rote learning typically involves no understanding of structure, chords, intervals etc. I believe that many experienced players retain hundreds or even thousands of tunes by using a wide variety of the tools including many of those described here. Good luck with the tunes!

Tune selection

Out of the many tunes that I play on the fiddle, it was a challenge to decide which tunes to select for this project. First, I chose tunes to represent a wide range of level of difficulty (from very easy to modestly difficult). Second, I chose many of the tunes because they provide very good examples of different bowing systems. For example, "Gray Cat on a Tennessee Farm" is a very simple tune which is great for beginners and an excellent introduction to the Nashville shuffle. I also included the ever so slightly more difficult "Barlow Knife" (in the key of D) and, a bit more difficult than "Barlow Knife," "Flop Eared Mule" as relatively easy examples using Nashville shuffle. I also chose tunes such as "Whiskey Before Breakfast" (a very good tune for 3-1 bowing since it has lots of eighth notes), "Fly Around my Pretty Little Miss" and others because they are standards that everyone knows. Alternately, I chose quite a few tunes because they are far less commonly played (e.g. "Hell Among the Stallions," "Road Dog," "Charles Guiteau," "Roscoe") and are among my favorites. Next, I chose a few tunes commonly played in altered tunings such as AEAE ("Hangman's") and ADAD. And I chose tunes to represent a range of keys/modes. In general, I stayed in the keys that are easiest to play on the fiddle (D, G and A major and A mixolydian.)

For new players: difficulty of tunes quick reference

I almost always start new players out with saw bowing and then the Nashville (basic) shuffle even though it isn't my primary "default" bowing pattern. It is, however, the easiest to learn, it works great to start and is still an important bowing. After practicing the simple shuffle, add drones, add the "touches" on adjacent strings and jump right into a tune. "Gray Cat on a Tennessee Farm" is the easiest tune with which to start. Then, try "Barlow Knife" and perhaps next "Flop Eared Mule." At that point, you should have the basic feel for Nashville shuffle. You can come back to Nashville shuffle as I include the pattern in other more complicated tunes ("Journey to the Heartland," "Hell Among the Stallions," "Road Dog") but I would then move to the simpler examples of 3-1 bowing. Some good starting tunes for 3-1 bowing include "Needle Case," "Shady Grove," "Julianne Johnson" and "Liza Jane." Each has at least some passages of 3-1 bowing. When you start to get the feel of the bowing system, move onto a tune with lots of eighth notes such as "Whiskey Before Breakfast." For "ghost bows," start with "Mike in the Wilderness." Plus, each part gives you something different to do. For the "rock," there are many examples. This is not an easy technique. You might want to start with "Puncheon Floor." There are plenty of tunes that offer many opportunities to work on chording ("Little Star" probably has the most if you really want to go at it!)

Below, I have tried to group the tunes based on difficulty. I find that players vary widely as to their experience with different tunes. Please consider this grouping as somewhat arbitrary. The number of stars indicates the difficulty level from one star (easiest) to five stars (hardest).

Nashville shuffle—in order of difficulty:

"Gray Cat on an Old Tennessee Farm" * (D) a very simple great beginning tune; add drones after you get the basic melody
"Barlow Knife" * (D) great beginning tune to learn Nashville shuffle; it is often played in the key of G
"Flop Eared Mule" ** (D/A) straightforward tune with Nashville shuffle including a few slurs
"Road Dog" *** (A) (AEAE) this includes a challenging use of Nashville shuffle
"Journey to the Heartland" **** (Dm/D) this tunes is more challenging as it uses Nashville shuffle, ghost bows and a section with a bow rock

"3-1 bowing"—these tunes are at about the same level of difficulty except for "Whiskey Before Breakfast" which is perhaps a little more challenging because it is very "notey."

"Needle Case" ** (D) very straightforward tune
"Julianne Johnson" ** (D) very good tune to start 3-1 bowing
"Single Footin' Horse" ** (D) simple, relatively easy tune
"Spotted Pony" ** (D) a standard and fairly easy
"Whiskey Before Breakfast" *** (D) a super standard tune, good for 3-1 bowing

Other relatively "easy" tunes:

"Liza Jane" ** (A) (AEAE or standard) straightforward, very sweet and lyrical tune
"Elk River Blues" ** (D but originally in G) I played this slowly with no chords and with chords and up to tempo without chords; timing is a bit tricky; good to work on your tone!
"Shady Grove" ** (A) (AEAE or standard) relatively easy tune. There are several tunes that go by this same name. This is not the one that most people know!

Mixed bowing, unison fourth finger, chords and other stuff —these are tough to order as the difficulty really varies from player to player, based on each individual's strengths and weaknesses):

"Mike in the Wilderness" *** (A) (AEAE) three parts with very different feels; features ghost bows, plucking
"Home with the Girls in the Morning" *** (Dm) powerful tune with mixed bowing; learned from my son
"Charleston Gals" *** (D mixolydian) good for 3-1 bowing and chording
"Roscoe" *** (G) a very sweet tune with some simple chording
"West Fork Gals" *** (D) an old standard and relatively straightforward
"Charles Guiteau" *** (G) simple tune and very good for working on ghost bows
"Shove that Pigs Foot a Little Bit Further in the Fire" *** (G) the title alone should make you want to learn this one!
"Hangman's" *** (A) (AEAE) a super standard and very good tune as a first for cross tuning
"Sandy Boys" **** (A mixolydian) (AEAE) a powerful tune; good to play cross tuned; good intro for working on fourth finger unisons and playing in two octaves with cross-tuning
"Puncheon Floor" **** (G/D) good for working on bow rocks
"Quince Dillon's High D" **** (D) look out for the C in the B part and especially for the high C sharp, I mean D, in the A part! Requires a position shift
"Richmond" **** (A mixolydian) (AEAE) great cross-tuned piece with a position shift
"Booth Shot Lincoln" **** (A) (AEAE) a beautiful and straightforward tune
"Fly Around My Pretty Little Miss" **** (D) simple tune with ghost bows, unison first and fourth fingering that makes this more challenging than expected
"Sally in the Garden" **** (Dm) lots of fun stuff here, especially holding the third finger while fingering other notes
"Hell Among the Stallions" **** (D) unusual crooked tune
"Little Star" ***** (G) played at one tempo only – challenging because of the use of chords; beautifully lyrical tune
"Ragtime Annie" ***** (D) bow rocks and 3-1 bowings, unison 1-4 fingering
"Devil in the Strawstack" ***** (Gm) (GDGD) Nashville shuffle and bow rocks
"Washington's March" ***** (D mixolydian) (ADAD) slur two and 3-1 patterns
"Chinquapin Huntin'" ***** (A) (AEAE) a great crooked tune; play it in two octaves; fourth finger unisons
"Big Sciota" ***** (G) some challenging chording in the B part

Barlow Knife

Traditional: Arranged by Ken Kolodner

This tune is usually played in the key of G but it works well in D especially for a more beginning tune. I have written out this tune using the Nashville shuffle exclusively. Other bowings are, of course, possible. But this is an excellent tune to work with the basic shuffle. A ⊓ indicates a down bow and a V indicates an up bow.

Once you master the basic tune, try adding an open string (drone) for each section. For the A section, play on the top two strings. While there will be some dissonance created by playing the D in the melody against the E string, this quickly resolves. Also, some dissonance is a good thing! In the A part, you may also add a first finger F♯ on the E string along with the D melody note which resolves the dissonance by providing a D chord. For the B and C sections, stay on the middle two strings to create a richer sound.

Tracks 4-6

Big Sciota

Traditional: Arranged by Ken Kolodner

For the first 4 measures in the A part, I hold down the third finger G throughout, until the triplet at the end of measure 4. In the first measure of the B part, hold the first finger on the A string to play a B against the melody up to the A in the second measure, at which point an open string A will suffice. The same idea can be used in the fifth measure of the B part (measure #14), except that here I bar the B and F♯ underneath the melody. In the third measure of the B part, I often play the first G as a G♯ but play the triplet that follows with a G natural.

For those of you interested in chords, I have suggested a progression that is not commonly played with this tune. But perhaps you will like to try it out. I especially like to play the descending line in the A part. In the B section, I would not play the B7 every time but it is a nice surprise to throw in every now and again. Some players will strongly object to the use of this chord but I like it! You will sometimes hear an Em at the top of the B part.

Booth Shot Lincoln

Tune AEAE or GDGD

Traditional: Arranged by Ken Kolodner

As in all cross-tuned pieces, most players make frequent use of drone strings. Since this tune uses all 4 strings, it is relatively easy to vary which drone string you use. This makes for different coloring of the piece. In the B part, in measures 10,14, and 18, use a 4th finger-open string unison. Note that in the recorded version, I often slide down from the F♯ to the open string E in measures 6, 15 and 23.

Reading music when cross-tuned is a bit tricky on the lower two strings. I strongly encourage listening to the tune first. You might try learning the tune in standard tuning, ignoring the bowing until you get the tune in your head.

Charles Guiteau

Traditional: Arranged by Ken Kolodner

I'm not sure why someone would choose to name a tune after Charles Guiteau, the guy who assassinated President Garfield, but at least it is a good one! This version comes from the playing of Wisconsin fiddler, Kevin McMullin.

In the A part measure 3, hold the third finger down to produce a chord against the G and F♯ that follow. In the last measure of the A part, add a B using the first finger on the A string. Hold the first finger down barred on the A and E string "underneath" the G, F♯ and G throughout the measure. In the B part first measure, I use a bunch of ghost bows. Also, hold the third finger G against the notes in measure 2 of the B part. In measure 3 of the part, I often use bow rocks (using a slur two pattern--not notated here.) In measure 6 of the B part, I play a first finger E against the C. In fact, you can again bar the D and A string, playing a first finger E against both the C and B in the measure.

Charleston Gals

Traditional: Arranged by Ken Kolodner

At the end of measure 2, I hold the third finger G down through the G on the second count in measure 4, releasing at the A. In the B part, I typically play a D chord on the 2 count of measure 1 by adding an F♯ (first finger on the E string). In the third measure of B part, I add a first finger E for the C chord. Elsewhere, open string drones are effective. I learned this version from Rhiannon Giddens while we were playing for a contra dance.

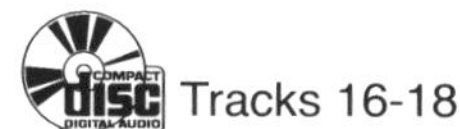

Chinquapin Hunting

Tuning: AEAE or standard

Traditional: Arranged by Ken Kolodner

This is a great "crooked tune." Musicians refer to tunes that have either an extra measure or a change in meter as "crooked" (see the extra measure of 2/4 in the A part). Since it resides completely on the top 2 strings (A and E), it is great for cross tuning. Move the tune to the lower octave and use the exact same fingering and bowing.

In measures 1, 2 and 3, while the tune works fine without doing so, I typically use unison 4th finger and open strings for the first two notes of each of the phrases. In the first measure of the B part, a ghost bow works well between the two up bows. In the first measure of the C part, try using a slight bow lift or release of bow pressure between the E and C♯. In the C part measure 1, many players add a third finger D to produce a D chord.

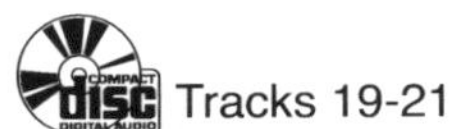
Tracks 19-21

Devil in the Strawstack

Tune GDGD

Traditional: Arranged by Ken Kolodner

Of course this great tune can be played in standard tuning but it is way more fun in cross tuning (GDGD). Use drone notes throughout the entire tune. Generally, I find it easier to learn cross tuning by listening. I would suggest listening first to get this one!

The chord in measure two is played by holding the 3rd finger down on the G string and placing the second finger on the F natural. To play the anticipation going into measure 3, I play two down bows in a row and leave a tiny space between the notes. I slightly lift the bow between the two down bows.

Measure 9 features a bow rock. Remember that because we are cross-tuned, the first two notes of the 9th measure can be played easily with the open strings. The bow rock in this measure uses the open string G (normally the A string!). Measure 13 is really the same measure as measure 9. However, instead of using a bow rock, to vary the tune, I add a syncopation in the beginning of the measure followed by an anticipation going into measure 14.

Tracks 22-24

Elk River Blues

Ernie Carpenter: Arranged by Ken Kolodner

Play both the D and A strings throughout except play a D drone only when melody drops below a low D. For example, play a D drone in measure 18. This tune is usually played in the key of G but I have heard it played in the key of A and D as well. It is clearly crooked and is more easily learned totally by ear. I have seen this tune written out all sorts of ways in terms of the timing. As always, but especially with this one, the bowing is a suggestion only. Really almost any bowing can work for this tune.

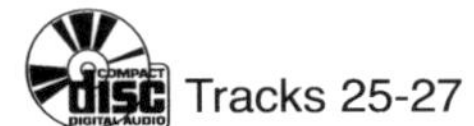

Flop Eared Mule

Traditional: Arranged by Ken Kolodner

This very commonly played tune is a good exercise for relative beginners to work with the Nashville shuffle and especially to work with a few measures of consecutive eighth notes (slurring two and then separating two). To greatly simplify learning this tune, note that measures three and four in both the A and B parts are identical except that you play on the D and then the A string, respectively. Measures seven and eight are also identical in both parts (but again played on different strings.) This is also a good tune with which drone strings may be added. Adjacent strings may be played throughout. In the entire B part, try using the A and E strings together. In the A part, the A and E strings can be played together when you are fingering on the E string. Otherwise, use the D and A strings. As an alternative to the constant use of drone strings, "touch" shuffle bowing can be used throughout. Simply hit the adjacent string only on the two and four counts.

Tracks 28-30

Fly Around My Pretty Little Miss

Traditional: Arranged by Ken Kolodner

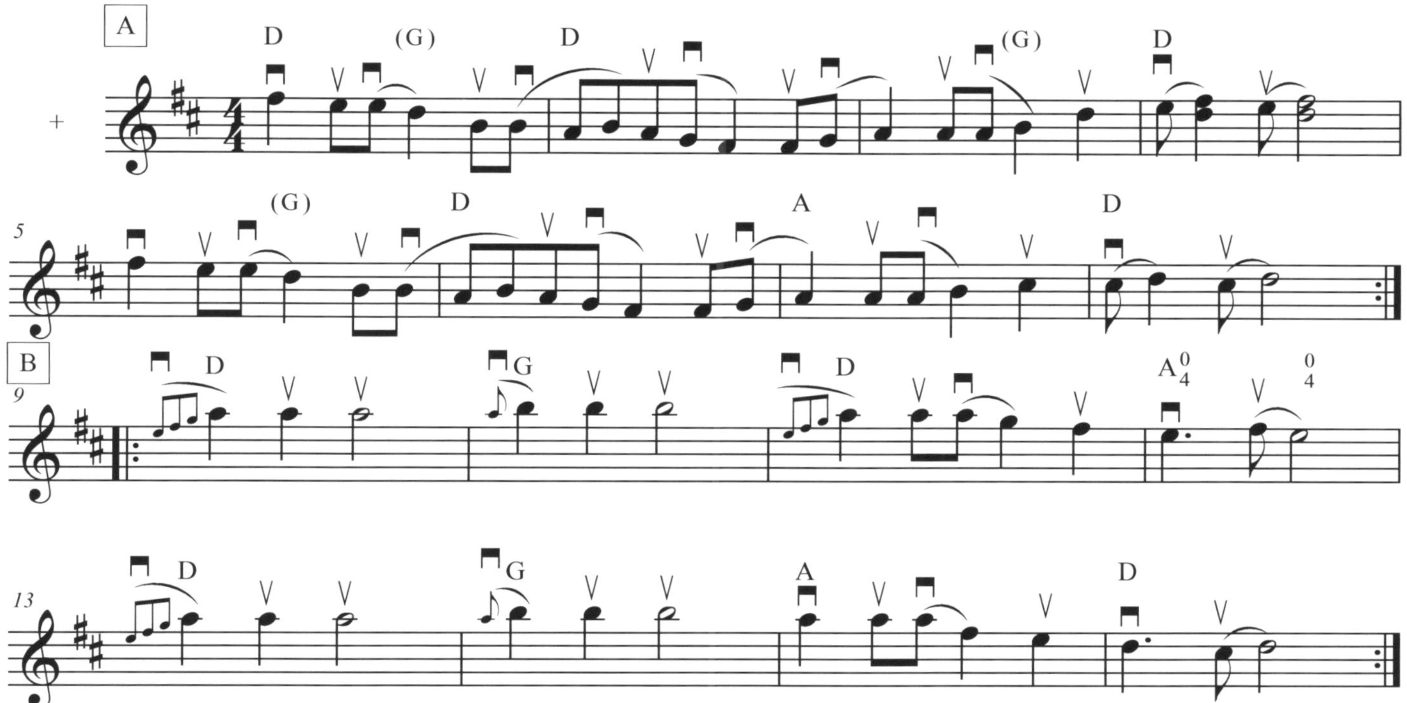

A part: At the end of measure 3, hold down the D and play it against the E and the F♯ in measure 4. B part: The triplets in measures 9, 11, 13 and 14 can be played in the same manner. However, I wrote out the triplets differently in measure 14 to indicate that you can choose to play them in a more relaxed fashion. Measures 9, 10, 13 and 14: In between the two consecutive "up bows," I typically play "ghost bows." I.e. play a down stroke "whisper" bow. Up to tempo, the ghost bow does not really produce any sound. These measures can be played many different ways including using the Nashville shuffle, bow rocks, etc. Measure 12: Use unison 4th finger and open E string. Keep the fourth finger down when playing the F♯. Measures 10 and 14: For an added challenge, use unison B's. I.e. place your first finger on the A string B and hold this down as you play the high B with your fourth finger. Throughout the tune, feel free to use adjacent string drone notes.

Gray Cat on an Old Tennessee Farm

Traditional: Arranged by Ken Kolodner

This very simple tune is a great place to start for complete beginners especially to work with the Nashville shuffle. Try first without any drone strings and then add an open string drone. Play the drone by staying completely on the middle two strings. Once mastered, try adding the fourth finger A (played on the D string) to produce a unison throughout the B part.

Tracks 34-36

Hangman's Reel

Tuning: AEAE or GDGD

Traditional Quebec/US: Arranged by Ken Kolodner

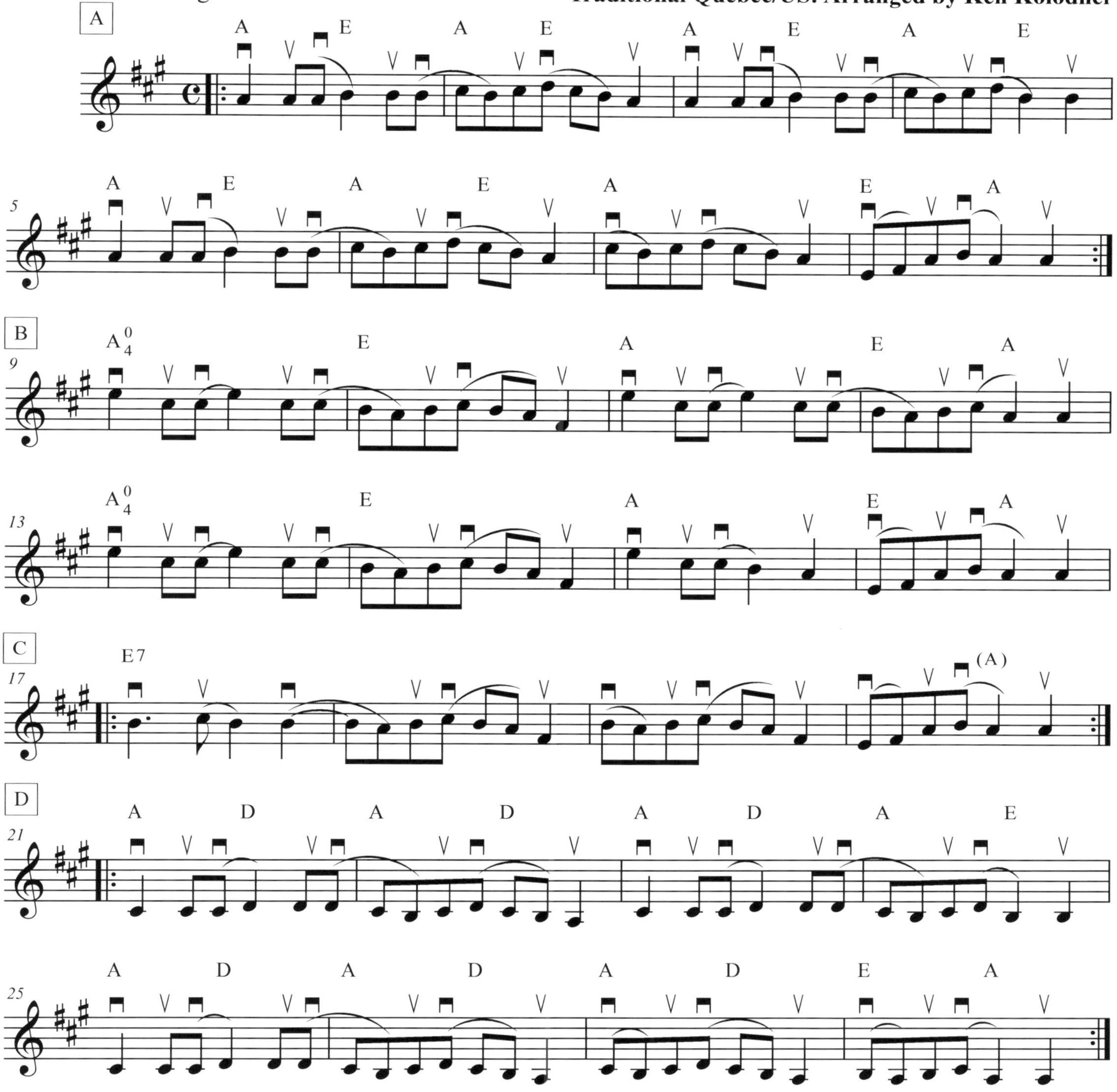

This is one of the "big" A tunes commonly played in old-time circles. (Among the many others are Little Billy Wilson, Camp Chase, Three Thin Dimes, Chinquapin Hunting). In the B part, the E can be played as an open string or a unison with the 4th finger. Despite having four parts, it is really quite straighforward! As with all tunes that are in cross-tuning, play drones throughout.

Hell Among the Stallions

Traditional: Arranged by Ken Kolodner

In this great "crooked" tune (with 9 measures in the A part), I enjoy mixing in several different bowing ideas including slur 2 patterns, longer slurs, Nashville shuffle, and 3-1 bowing. In measures 3-4 in the B part (and measures 13-14), bar the first finger on the G and D string. Some players may prefer to tune the G string up to an A (i.e. ADAE). In so doing, barring is no longer needed.

Tracks 40-42

Home with the Girls in the Morning

Standard tuning or ADAD

Traditional: Arranged by Ken Kolodner

A

Dm C Dm Am

5

Dm C C Am Dm

B

9

Dm Am Dm Am Dm C Dm

13

Dm Am Dm Am C Am Dm

17

Dm Am Dm Am Dm C D

21

Dm Am Dm Am C Am Dm

In this wonderful tune, I use both Nashville shuffle and 3-1 bowing to provide a nice contrast in groove. Watch out for the surprise F♯ (D major chord) in the B part!! This tune also sounds great in ADAD. I chose to play it in standard tuning here. If you try ADAD, rather than using your first finger in the B part for the chords, the open string will do the job (easier!). And in the A part, use your high open D string (formerly your E string) as a drone note as much as you desire. I learned this tune from my son.

Journey to the Heartland

Recorded on Ken Kolodner's 2005 recording "Journey to the Heartland"

Ken Kolodner

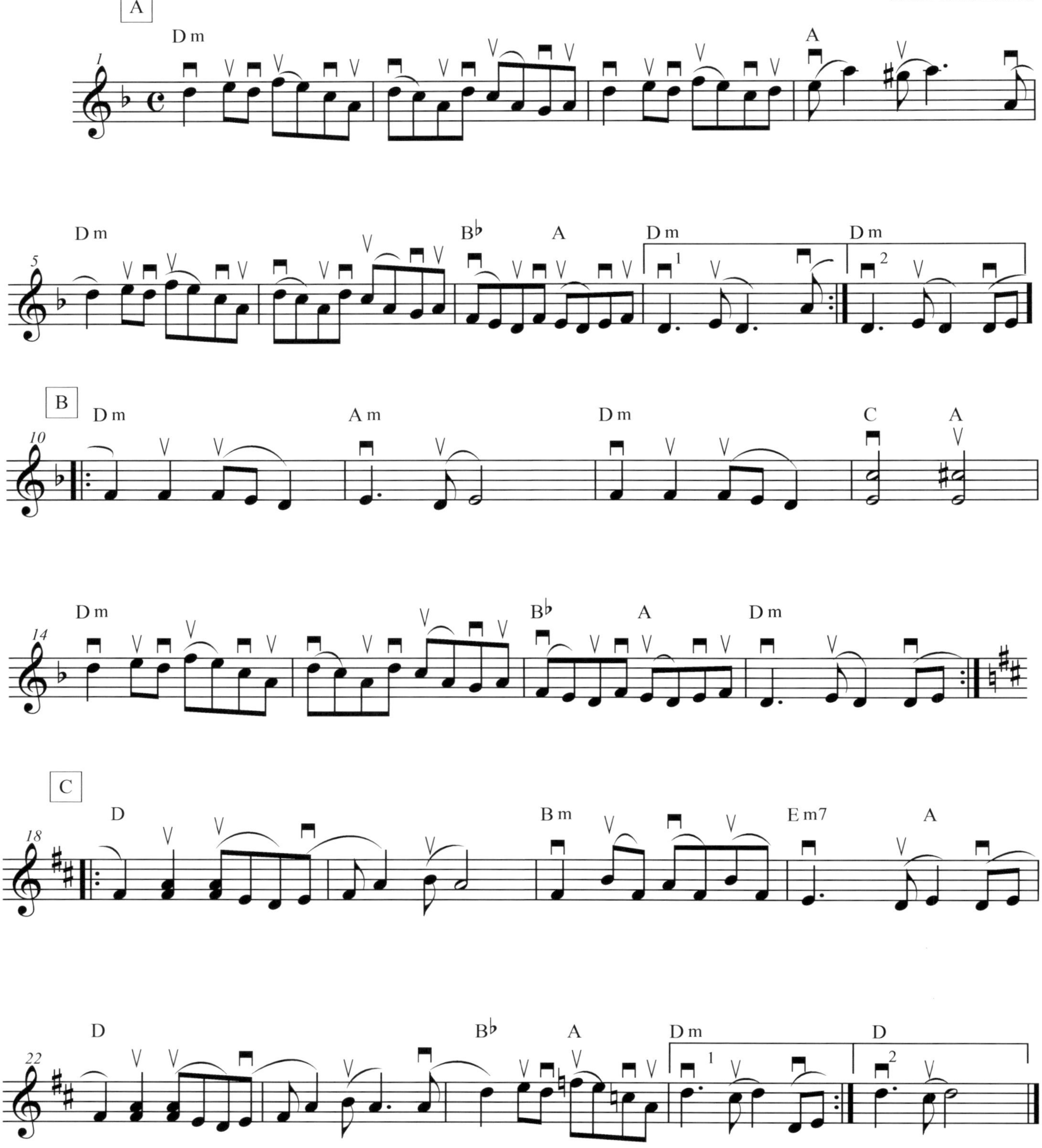

For a good part of this tune, I suggest using the simple or basic shuffle (Nashville shuffle). I add drone strings in the last two measures of the A part and in the first three measures of the B part. The "bow rock" in the C part is a little tricky. While this section can be played with single bows, the slur pattern makes for a smooth phrasing. Be careful with the C part moving to D major.

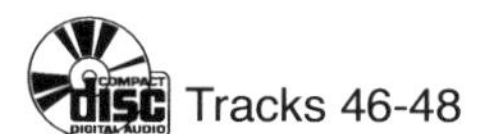

Julianne Johnson

Traditional: Arranged by Ken Kolodner

The repetitive phrases in this tune make it a very suitable as a good introduction for 3-1 bowing. In the A part, in measure 3, I do not play a ghost bow between the two up bows but rather simply play two up bows. For those paying attention to chords, you may elect to resolve the tune back to a D chord. This tune is very widely played in old time circles.

Track 49

Little Star

Traditional: Arranged by Ken Kolodner

This is an unusual and super tune from the wonderful bowed dulcimer playing of Ken Bloom. I have changed it a bit but it is close enough! It is a great one for working on chords. Consequently, I wrote in many of the chords this time. Since this tune is very melodic and does not have a strong rhythmic feel, the bowing is not that vital to make the tune work. But don't play it too fast!

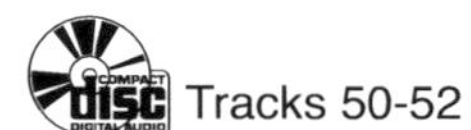

Tracks 50-52

Liza Jane

Traditional: Arranged by Ken Kolodner

This beautifully lyrical tune works well in standard or in cross-tuning (AEAE). There are a bunch of tunes that share the name Liza Jane but this is my favorite! In the fourth measure of the A part, I often hold the C♯ from the previous measure and play a chord with the E and the F♯ in measure 4, thus suggesting an F♯m chord. Drones can be added throughout the tune. For the ending A in both the A and B parts, I play a unison A either with the fourth finger (if playing in standard) or with your third finger (if cross-tuned).

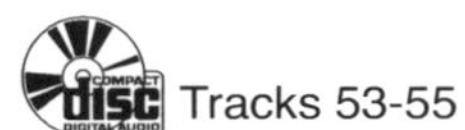

Mike in the Wilderness

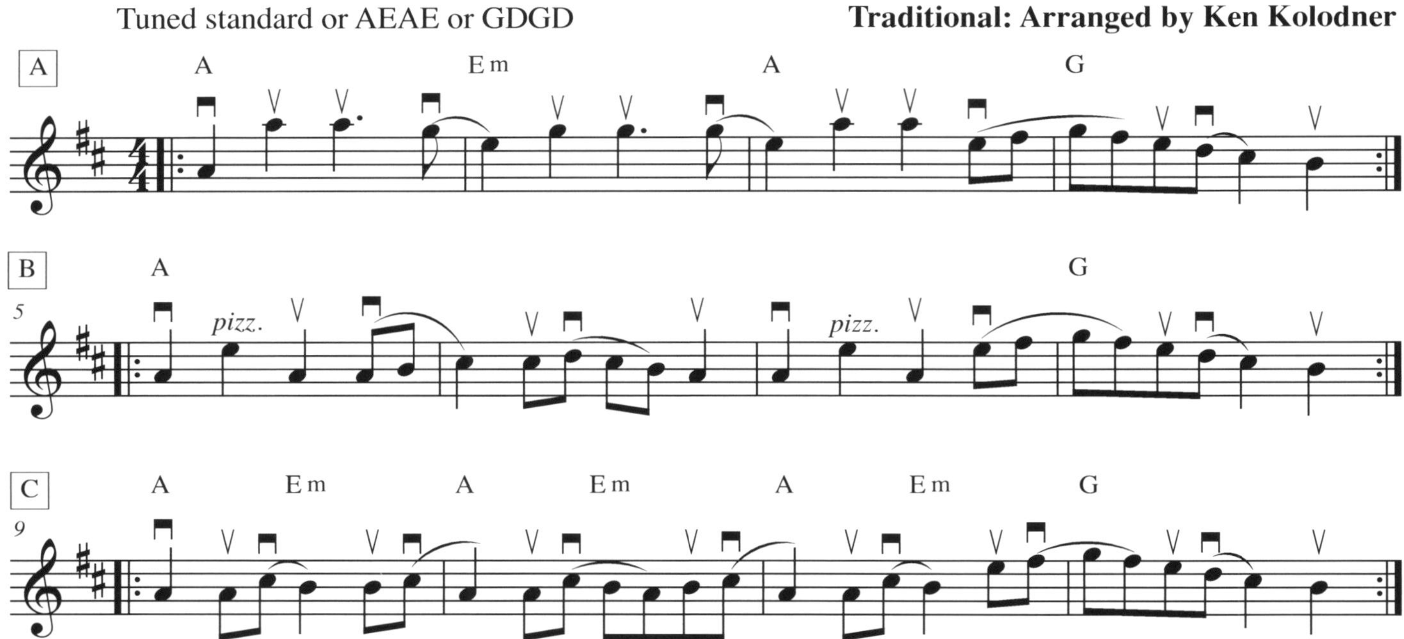

Since the tune resides completely on the top two strings, this tune can be easily moved to the lower two strings (when cross-tuned). In measure 2 of the A part, I sometimes play an open A against the G melody notes and at other times I play a G chord by placing my first finger on the B on the A string. Both approaches work. I mostly use drone strings throughout the tune. On the recorded versions, note the triplets in the A part. The "pizz" can be played by plucking the E string with either the third or fourth finger on the left hand. Pick up the bow while playing the pizzicato. Note that the endings in each part are exactly the same but that the bowing changes slightly in the C part.

Needle Case

Traditional: Arranged by Ken Kolodner

This very widely played tune is a relatively easy one for introducing 3-1 bowing. In measures two and six in the A part, hold the first finger B and second finger G down to produce a G chord. The chord progression in the A and B parts are conveniently identical!

Puncheon Floor

Traditional: Arranged by Ken Kolodner

You might want to end this tune by returning to at least one A part. Adding a drone string by going to the next lower string is effective but I try not to hang on the drone all the time and just use it periodically for contrast. Note the use of some "3-1" bow patterns (where we slur three and then have one single bow).

In the A part, I am using ghost bows between the consecutive "up" bows. In the B part, I am using several alternate bowing ideas to essentially play the same phrase. The first three measures of the B part use a simple bowing. In measure five of the B part, I have suggested using a bow "rock" instead. And Nashville shuffle would suffice as well. I vary the bowing significantly through this tune. However, you might want to stick with one consistent way until you have the tune very solidly in the groove.

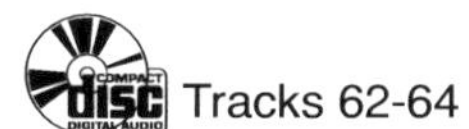

Quince Dillon's High D

Traditonal: Arranged by Ken Kolodner

Look out for the position shift in the A part. Many fiddlers like to slide into the shift using the first finger to slide up to the A. It makes for a nice effect and is perhaps less scary to do in case you are worrying about finding the note. In the B part, make sure you play a low second finger (C natural) in the third measure.

Ragtime Annie

Traditional: Arranged by Ken Kolodner

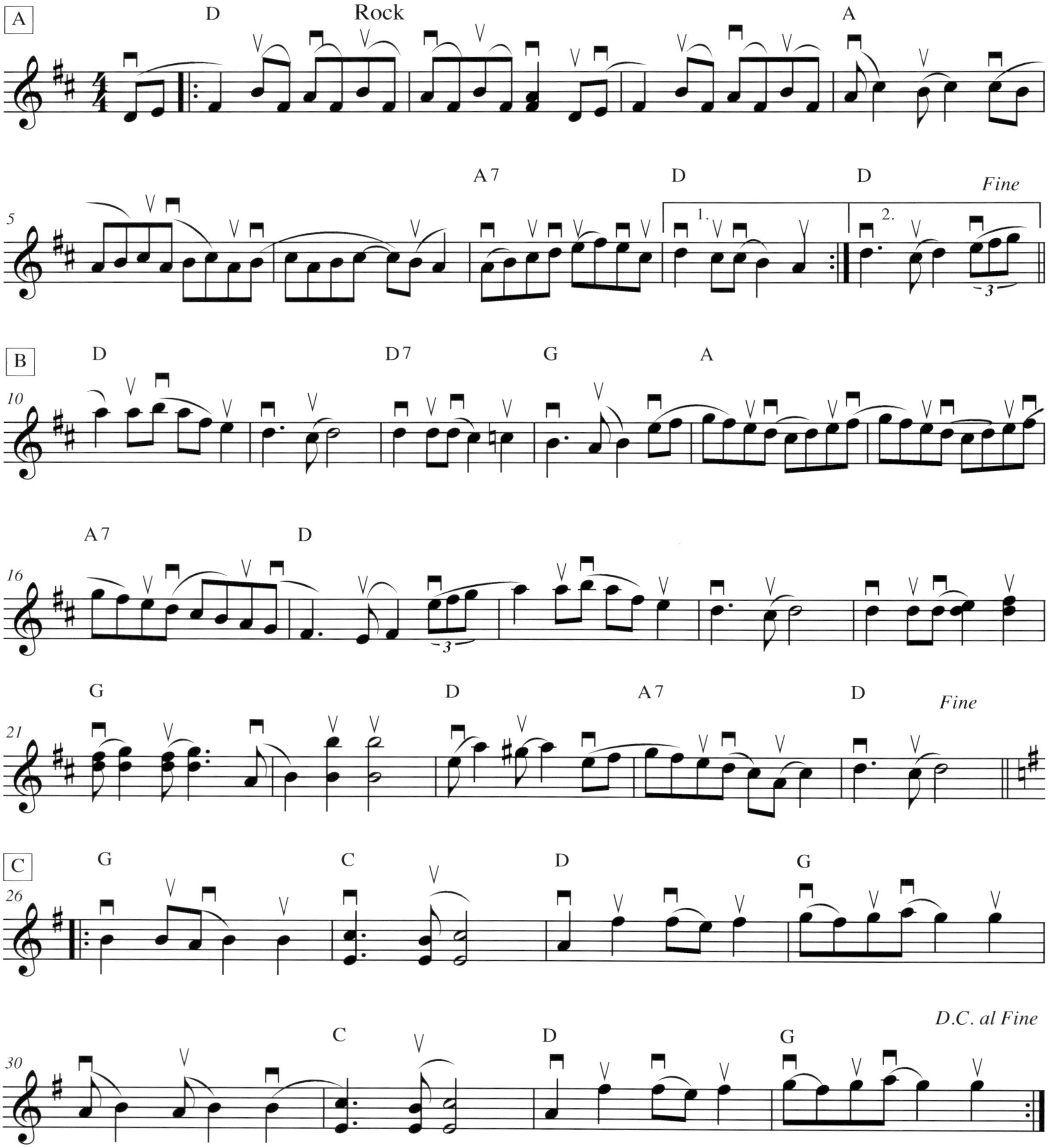

There is often debate among players whether to play the C part or not. In fact, there is considerable debate what the notes of the C part actually are as the "melody" is really just a collection of a few chords from which many players enjoy improvising. I offer these notes in the C part as a general guide. When playing the tune with the C part included, many players will end on the B part.

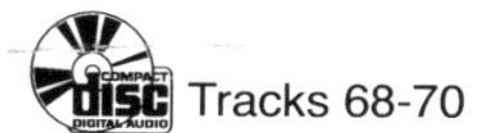 Tracks 68-70

Richmond

Tuning: AEAE

Traditional: Arranged by Ken Kolodner

[A]

A E A

5

G D E A E A

[B]

9

A 1 1 3 G D A

13

A G D E A E A

In measure 3 of the A part, I hold the first finger on the A string (to play the B) along with the second finger on the D string (but tuned up to E) to get a G♯. Hold these fingers throughout the measure and play as a chord. In the B part, sliding up to the position shift while playing an open A is a highlight of the tune! Watch for anticipations throughout the tune but especially in the B part. When cross-tuned, this great crooked piece can be played easily in the lower octave but you will have to slightly modify the A part as you no longer will have a low G♯.

Tracks 71-73

Road Dog

Tuning: AEAE or standard

Traditional: Arranged by Ken Kolodner

I primarily use Nashville shuffle in this wonderful tune, along with some "saw" bowing and the occassional long slur for variety. I tend to vary the bowing constantly in this tune but this should provide a reasonable start! The source for this tune is probably Steve Hickman.

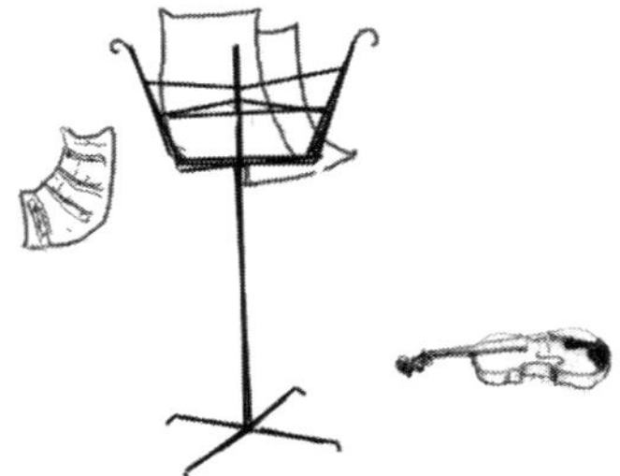

Tracks 74-76

Roscoe

Traditional: Arranged by Ken Kolodner

As this tune is very lyrical and sweet rather than highly rhythmic, it seems to lend itself to many options in terms of bowing. I rarely bow it consistently and would be hard pressed to duplicate even what I have written here, unless I look at it! Feel free to experiment (as always).

In the A part, in measure two, I suggest using two down bows in a row and put a bit of a breath between the notes. In the A part, I use chords sparingly and reserve them for the appearance of the C chord in measure six (holding the first finger E on the string). In measures 10 and 11 (the first two measures in the B part), note that I hold the third finger G down throughout the measures. In fact, I don't release the G until near the end of the next measure.

Regarding the chord choices, the tune can be played easily using fairly obvious G, C and D chords only. These chords might get you kicked out of some jams but I like the bassline! This tune comes to me via Greg Canote.

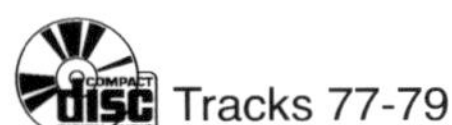

Sally in the Garden

Traditional: Arranged by Ken Kolodner

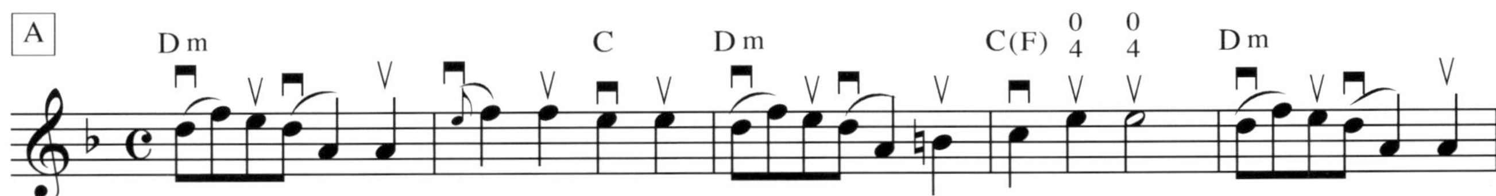

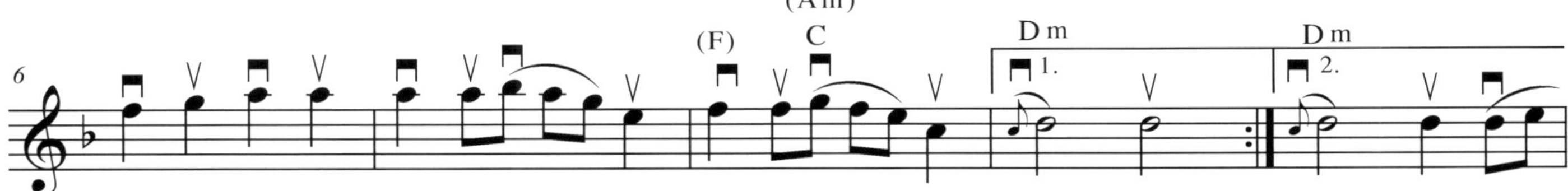

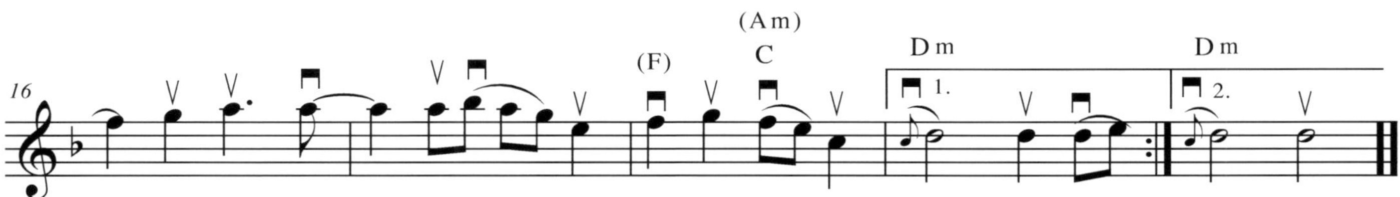

In measures two and six of the A part, a bow rock using an open A string works great. In measure three, I often slide the fourth finger up to the unison E and back down to at least a D. In the first two measures of the B part, I hold the third finger D down against the melody until the high A in the second measure. I again use the D through the third measure and throughout the fourth measure. Try playing the whole tune one octave lower.

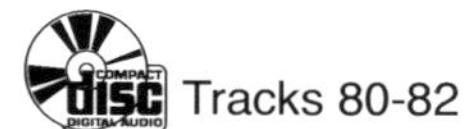

Tracks 80-82

Sandy Boys

Tuning: AEAE or standard

Traditional: Arranged by Ken Kolodner

As this tune resides entirely on the top two strings, this is an easy tune to play in the lower octave if played cross-tuned (AEAE or GDGD). At the first ending, I have notated the triplet with a G♯. Since the note goes by quickly, it really doesn't matter that much whether you play a G or G♯ but I do like to vary which I use. The G♯ in measure three of the A part can be played with the second finger or by sliding the third finger.

In measures one, two, five and six of the B part, use fourth finger and open string unisons on the E. Moving into the second measure of the B part, I often play the anticipation as indicated, but sometimes I will play it without the anticipation (as indicated in measures five and six of the B part). And other times, I might play the section with more of a shuffle feel. In measures two and six of the B part, I typically use ghost bows between the two up bows.

This is one of the mostly widely played tunes in A mixolydian. No one seems to ever tire of playing it!

Tracks 83-85

Shady Grove

Tuning: standard or AEAE

Traditional: Arranged by Ken Kolodner

This is a straightforward tune that can be played easily in two otaves without changing your fingering (if cross-tuned). There is nothing mysterious here. This is not the Shady Grove that many people know as a song.

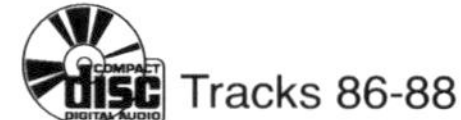

Tracks 86-88

Shove That Pigs Foot a Little Further in the Fire

Traditional: Arranged by Ken Kolodner

I use Nashville shuffle in the A part in this transcription. However, I never stick with this bowing for very long. While I wrote out the anticipations in the A part, another way to vary the tune is to sometimes use the anticipations and sometimes just play it straight. In measure two and five of the B part, I hold the D against the G and F♯ that follow. Otherwise, adjacent lower drone strings work well throughout.

Tracks 89-91

Single Footin' Horse

Traditional: Arranged by Ken Kolodner

This is a very straightforward tune. In the fourth measure of the B part, I usually play a unison fourth finger rather than open strings. However, I often play the notes E, F♯ and E in this measure in a lower octave. I learned this tune from Neal Walters.

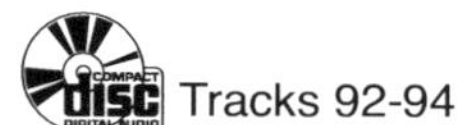

Tracks 92-94

Spotted Pony

Traditional: Arranged by Ken Kolodner

A

B

Alternate B part

This is a very widely played tune that is not too terribly hard to play. I add a "ghost bow" in between each of the two consecutive up bows throughout the tune. Measures 1-3 and 5-7 work well droning on the A string. In measure four, play the A string as a drone. In measure eight, you may drone use the open A for the F♯ and E notes and end with an open D string for the ending note D. Similar use of open strings can work throughout the B part. The alternate B part is more "notey" and uses 3-1 bowing throughout. I offer this as an example of how to vary your playing. I also prefer the alternate B part. The minor chords are not usually played.

Washington's March

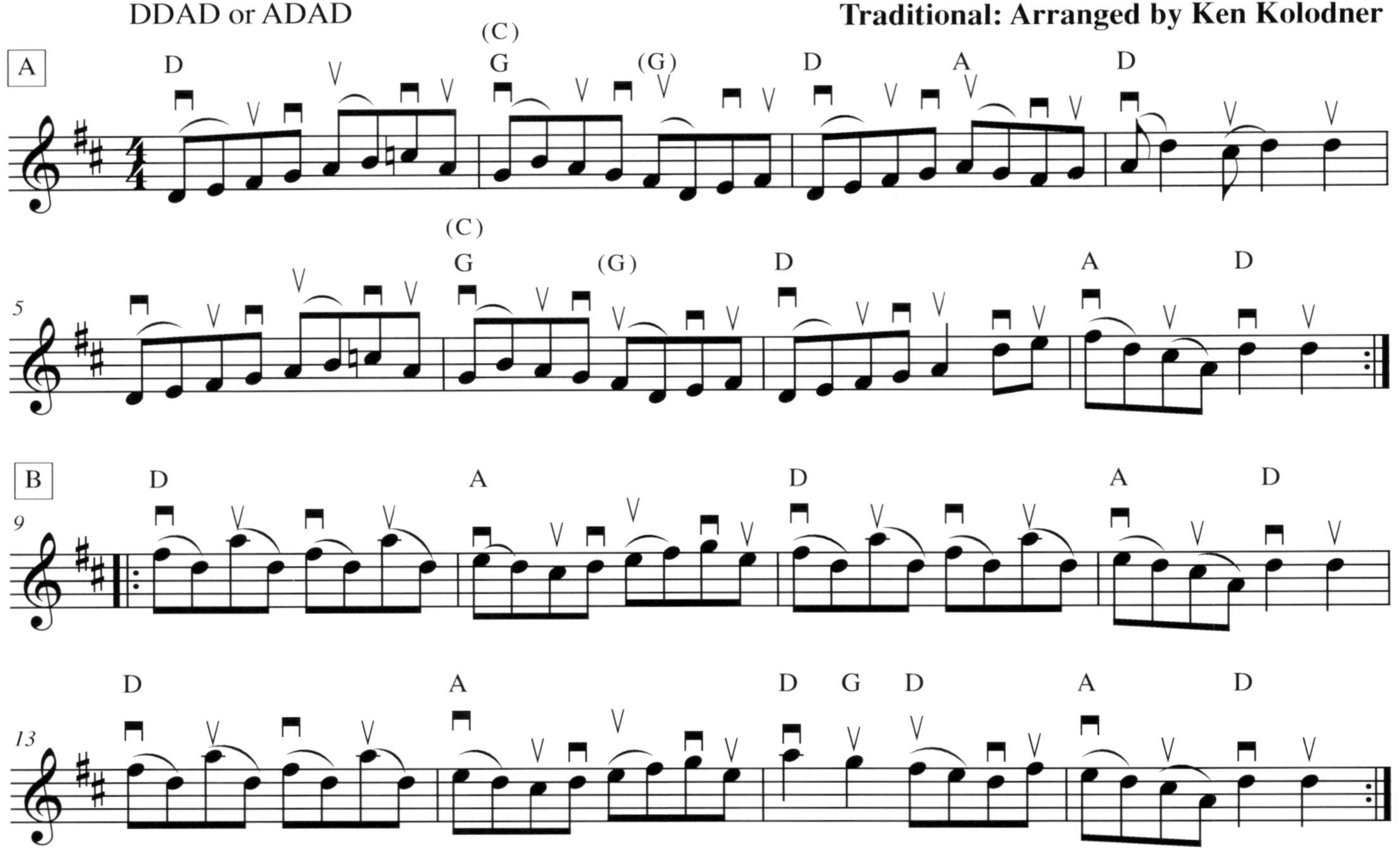

While I use primarily Nashville shuffle in the A part, I change the groove in the B part by using a slur-two pattern along with the occasional Nashville shuffle and a ghost bow in measure 15. By using the ADAD tuning, it is relatively easy to move the B part down an octave for a nice effect. In the A part measure one, I keep the G down through the remainder of the measure into the second measure. In measure four of the A part, I play the two consecutive up bows with a slight stop between the notes.

Tracks 98-100

West Fork Gals

Traditional: Arranged by Ken Kolodner

This is a widely played but fun tune with nothing too mysterious in the bowing.

Tracks 101-103

Whiskey Before Breakfast

Traditional: Arranged by Ken Kolodner

A

D (G) D G D A

D (G) D G D A D

B

D (Bm) A (Em) A *

D A G D G D A7 D

* Alternate for first line of B section

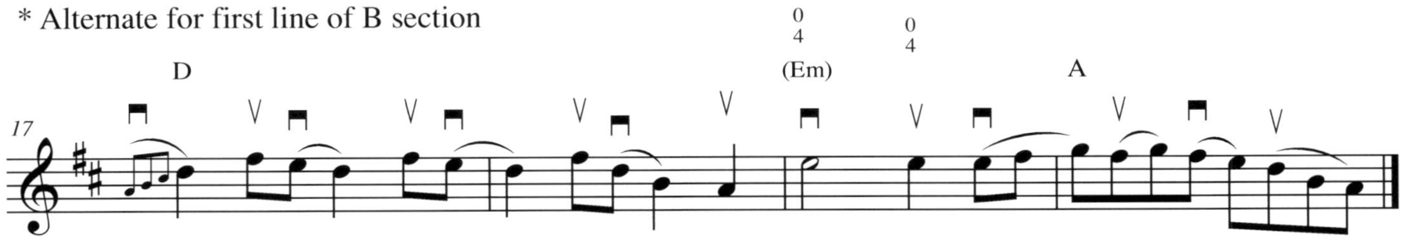

D (Em) A

I have written out this super standard tune using mostly 3-1 bowing, making it an excellent tune to nail down the bowing style. Try reversing the bow direction and obtain the same effect.

Index of tunes

Barlow Knife 22
Big Sciota 23
Booth Shot Lincoln 24
Charles Guiteau 25
Charleston Gals 26
Chinquapin Hunting 27
Devil in the Strawstack 28
Elk River Blues 29
Flop Eared Mule 30
Fly Around My Pretty Little Miss 31
Gray Cat on an Old Tennessee Farm 32
Hangman's Reel 33
Hell Among the Stallions 34
Home with the Girls in the Morning 35
Journey to the Heartland 36
Julianne Johnson 37
Little Star 38
Liza Jane 39
Mike in the Wilderness 40
Needle Case 41
Puncheon Floor 42
Quince Dillon's High D 43
Ragtime Annie 44
Richmond 45
Road Dog 46
Roscoe 47
Sally in the Garden 48
Sandy Boys 49
Shady Grove 50
Shove That Pigs Foot a Little Bit Further in the Fire 51
Single Footin' Horse 52
Spotted Pony 53
Washington's March 54
West Fork Gals 55
Whiskey Before Breakfast 56

About the author

Based in Baltimore, MD, Ken Kolodner has played old-time fiddle for nearly 30 years. He is also widely regarded as a major influence in the rebirth of the hammered dulcimer in the U.S., hailed as "one of today's most accomplished, musical hammered dulcimer artists..." (*Elderly*). As a soloist and in ensembles with Helicon (with Chris Norman and Robin Bullock), Greenfire (with Laura Risk), with Elke Baker, Jim Eagan and many others, Ken has performed and taught extensively for over 25 years. Focusing largely on traditional music, he is a regular fixture at many music camps and festivals (e.g. Common Ground, Swannanoa Gathering, Meadowlark, Augusta, Kentucky Music Week, and The John Campbell Folk School). Ken has been featured numerous times on NPR, *The Thistle and the Shamrock*, *All Things Considered,* the CBC, the Voice of America and German National Radio. Among his many credits are a featured solo in an Emmy-nominated CBS-TV Christmas special, five instructional CDs on the hammered dulcimer, ten recordings with sales well over 125,000, including an "Indie" winner (Helicon's "A Winter Solstice Celebration", winner of Best Seasonal Recording in 1999), and a #1 World Music title ("Walking Stones") and bestseller for BMG (with over 55,000 copies sold). Ken's playing has been described as "nothing short of astonishing" (*The Connection*), "outstanding" (*The New York Times*), "marvelous" (*The Washington Post*), "virtuosic" (*Audio*), "stunning in its musicality" (*Dulcimer Player News*) and "not to be missed" (*USA TODAY*). Ken has recently added the hammered mbira to his concert performances. Ken has two recordings to be released in 2010: a recording of Old-Time music with his son Brad Kolodner (clawhammer banjo and guitar) and another of Celtic, Quebecois and Old-Time music with fiddler Elke Baker.

Selected Discography:

Daybreak, Chris Norman and Ken Kolodner, JEB 001, 1985, JEB Records, re-released, FENCHURCH MUSIC, 2009.
Helicon (with Chris Norman and Robin Bullock), JEB 002, 1987, Jeb Records.
The Titan, Helicon, DORIAN Discovery, DIS-80115, 1989, re-released, JEB-003, 2006.
Horizons, Helicon, DORIAN Discovery, DIS-80103, 1992.
Walking Stones: A Celtic Sojourn, Ken Kolodner with Laura Risk and Robin Bullock, DORIAN, DOR-90248, 1997, Re-released FENCHURCH MUSIC, 2006.
Greenfire, A Celtic String Ensemble (Ken Kolodner, Laura Risk and Robin Bullock), DORIAN, DOR-90321, 1998.
A Winter Solstice Celebration, Helicon (With Chris Norman and Robin Bullock), DORIAN, DOR-90531, 1999.
A Roof for the Rain, Greenfire, (Ken Kolodner, Laura Risk, with guests Keith Murphy and Joseph Sobel) DORIAN, DOR-90598, 2001.
A Journey to the Heartland, Ken Kolodner (with guests Laura Risk, Elke Baker, Robin Bullock, Paddy League) MAGGIE'S MUSIC, MM231, 2005.

Selected other recordings on which Ken appears:

Christmas Gifts: A Dorian Sampler, DORIAN, DOR-90321, 1998.
Highlands Chris Norman, DORIAN, DOR-90321, 1997.
Glenelg: Variations in Light and Shade, Elke Baker, 2001.
The Road from Erin, Various artists, DORIAN, DOR-90021, 2002.
A Reason to Dance, Rick Thum, 2001.
Dulcianna, A Southwest Dulcimer, Anna Duff, 2001.
Jiggle the Handle, Samantha Oberkfell, 2005.
The Preacher's Daughters, Rachel Sprinkel and Deb Justice, 2005.
International Hackbrett Festival, Volume I, Various Artists, 2005.
On a Meadowlark Night, Eric Reiner, 2009.

Books:

Traditional Music from Ireland, Scotland, Quebec and Beyond: Tunes from Roof for the Rain and Greenfire, Fenchurch Music, 2002.

Instructional CDs by Ken Kolodner (Fenchurch Music):

Hammered Dulcimer Arrangements: Fiddle Tunes (Reels), Volume I, 2004.
Hammered Dulcimer Arrangements: Waltzes and Slow Tunes, Volume I, 2004.
Hammered Dulcimer Arrangements: Fiddle Tunes (Reels) Volume II, 2005.
Hammered Dulcimer Arrangements: Waltzes and Slow Tunes, Volume II, 2005.
Hammered Dulcimer Arrangements: Seasonal Music, Volume I, 2005.

www.kenkolodner.com